JOYCE'S DUBLIN
A Walking Guide to
Ulysses

To my parents, Robin, Megan, John and Kaitlin

ACKNOWLEDGEMENTS AND CREDITS

JACK McCARTHY is a lawyer, real estate developer and author living and working in Princeton, New Jersey. He is a 1969 graduate of Princeton University (highest honors in history) and a 1973 graduate of the University of Pennsylvania Law School. A frequent visitor to Ireland, he was also the founder of the first cable television system in the Princeton area and was the co-executive producer of the video *Walking into Eternity: James Joyce's Ulysses – A Dublin Tour with Patrick Ryan* directed by Seán Ó Mórdha. He is married with three children.

Maps: Bob Conrad
New Photographs: Peter Harding
Administration: Susan Jabanoski
Word Processing: Patty Cherrington
and Beth Marbach
Editors of the first edition: Abigail Bok and
Loretta Byrne
Index map pp. 8-9 adapted from first edition
map by E. Ryan

Thanks to Joyce Scholars:

Peter Costello	Dublin
Don Gifford	Williams College
Clive Hart	University of Essex
Walton Litz	Princeton University
David Norris	Trinity College Dublin
John O'Hanlon	Dublin
Sean J. White	School of Irish Studies

Thanks to:
The Society of Authors as literary representatives of the Estate of James Joyce for permission to quote from *Ulysses*.

Ordnance Survey of Ireland, Phoenix Park, for permission to reproduce maps of Dublin – Permit No. 4127.

National Library of Ireland for permission to reproduce photographs from the Lawrence Collection.

Special Thanks:
Joe Marshall, Patrick H. Ryan, Sean Waldron and Paul Gray.

JOYCE'S DUBLIN
A Walking Guide to
Ulysses

JACK McCARTHY

with
DANIS ROSE

*An extensively revised and rewritten edition,
with additional maps and photographs*

WOLFHOUND PRESS

1988 edition
Text, maps and new pictures
© Jack McCarthy 1986, 1988

Archive pictures from the Lawrence Collection
National Library, Dublin.

First edition 1986.
This revised edition 1988 published by Wolfhound Press,
68 Mountjoy Square, Dublin 1

British Library Cataloguing in Publication Data

McCarthy, Jack
Joyce's Dublin: A walking guide to *Ulysses* — New ed.
1. Fiction in English. Joyce, James, 1882-1941.
Local associations : Dublin
I. Title
823'.912

ISBN 0-86327-169-3

Cover design by Jan de Fouw
Cover photos: *front* Peter Zöller; *back* Bórd Fáilte
Typesetting and Origination by Redsetter Ltd
Printed by The Leinster Leader, Ireland

CONTENTS

INTRODUCTION

James Joyce (1882-1941) once remarked that he was 'more interested in the street names of Dublin than in the riddle of the universe'. Dublin is a detailed presence in all of Joyce's works, but his classic novel *Ulysses*, published in 1922, put Dublin on the literary map and earned enduring fame for many Dublin places. *Ulysses* follows the wanderings of Stephen Dedalus, Leopold Bloom and other local characters through Dublin on a single day – June 16, 1904 – known to Joyceans since the publication of *Ulysses* as 'Bloomsday'. On this day Joyce may have had his first date with his wife, Nora Barnacle. Joyce's father, hearing that his son had run off to the Continent with a woman named Barnacle, quipped, 'Well, she'll stick to him anyway'.

This book traces the routes that the main characters in *Ulysses* take through Dublin. Joyce makes it difficult for the reader to follow such paths. He even bragged about putting so many 'enigmas and puzzles' in *Ulysses* that it would keep the professors busy for centuries. This book is an attempt to clarify one aspect of Joyce's puzzle – which characters took what paths in Dublin. It is written for general readers (not the specialists) who want to see the city for themselves and follow in the footsteps of Stephen and Bloom – climbing the Martello Tower, walking Sandymount Strand, drinking at Davy Byrne's Pub or reading in the National Library.

Like *Ulysses*, this book is divided into eighteen chapters. I have briefly described some of the 'stage action' (as author Anthony Burgess calls it) of the book with particular emphasis on what places can still be seen today (often indicated by boldface).

GENERAL SUGGESTIONS

Walking. Joyce spent hours strolling through Dublin – many of his dates with Nora were walks. The best way to learn about Joyce's Dublin is on foot, carrying a copy of this book. The Irish Tourist Board offices at 14 Upper O'Connell Street (telephone 747733) sometimes keeps a list of guides offering special Joycean walks through Dublin. Tom Buggy (386485) and Rose Johnson (947242) are two Joyceans who offer such guided tours, and during the Bloomsday festivities the James Joyce Institute of Ireland often advertises organized walking tours.

Driving. Driving combined with walking is the fastest way to see Joycean landmarks. Try to avoid driving yourself if you are not a native; Dublin's maze of one way streets can be confusing; however, Irish motorists are generally courteous and Irish people are helpful (if somewhat vague) about directions. Just keep to the left, drive slowly, and watch out for Americans driving on the wrong side of the road.

Dublin taxis, unlike their London counterparts, are a mixed bag. Asking for certain Joycean destinations you will often get a blank stare. A five-mile journey will cost about £8 – £9 ($14 – $15); tip £1 ($1.60). You can usually negotiate a two-hour taxi tour of Dublin for approximately £26 ($42). Driving is also the quickest way to follow the funeral procession, Father Conmee's walk (and tram ride) and the viceregal cavalcade, and see such 'suburban' Joycean landmarks as Glasnevin Cemetery, the O'Brien Institute, Phoenix Park and the RDS.

For the elegant Joycean tour, a chauffeur-driven Mercedes will run about £125 (or $200) per day. Neville Breen (480678) is one driver familiar with some of the Joycean trails. The Irish Tourist Board (747733) often has a list of companies providing chauffeur-driven car service.

Buses.   A more leisurely and less costly way to see Joyce's Dublin is from the top of a multi-coloured Dublin bus. Like their red counterparts in London, Dublin's double-decker buses offer a wonderful view of the city and its people. Be sure to go to the end of any waiting line (queue), take a seat, tell the conductor your final destination and pay the fare based on zones. Dublin bus conductors are usually courteous, outgoing and eager to help a lost Joycean. The front of each bus is marked with the bus number and final destination. Some particular Joycean routes are Nos. 2 and 3 (Sandymount) from O'Connell Street to Leahy's Terrace, which cover much of the funeral route, and No. 22 (Cabra West to Dolphin's Barn) which passes through much of the city of Joyce's childhood, north and south.

DART.   The Dublin Area Rapid Transit (DART) is a fast, easy and safe way to see a surprising number of Joycean landmarks. The DART is a single line running on a frequent basis along the old Howth to Bray railroad line. The twenty-five DART stations are clearly marked. I have listed the appropriate DART stop at the beginning of each chapter.

Museums.   The best known Joyce landmark is Joyce's Tower Museum run by the Irish Tourist Board. It contains one of the finest collections of Joyceana in the world – books, letters, photographs and souvenirs. The curator, Robert Nicholson, an eminent Joyce scholar, stocks everything from lemon-scented soap to reproductions of the Martello tower key. Joyce's Tower is open from May to September, Monday through Saturday 10 a.m. to 1 p.m., 2 p.m. to 5 p.m. and Sunday 2.30 p.m. to 6 p.m.; and from October to April by appointment (telephone 808571).

Scheduled to open in 1991 is the James Joyce Cultural Centre at 35 North Great George's Street. Founded by Ireland's best-known Joycean, Senator David Norris, the restored Georgian townhouse will include a complete set of Joyce family portraits and other Joyceana.

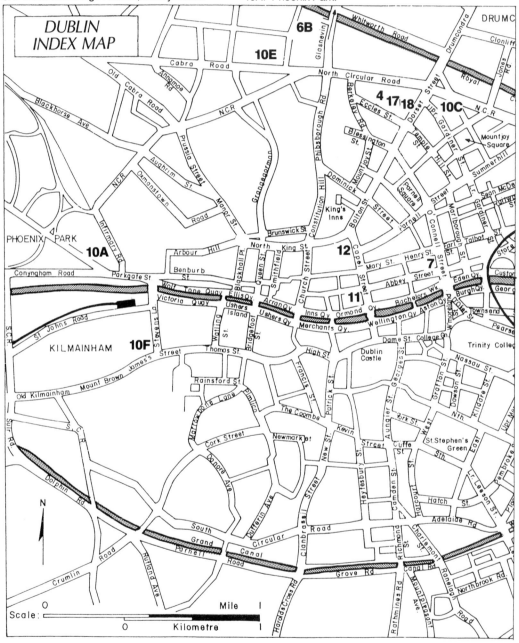

10B: R D S, Ballsbridge.

10C: Presbytery, Gardiner Street.

10D: O'Brien Institute, Artane.

10E: Joyce's Home, No. 7 St. Peter's Terrace.

10F: Sundial, James's Street.

11: Ormond Hotel on the Liffey, Upper Ormond Quay.

12: Barney Kiernan's Pub, Little Britain Street.

13: Sandymount Strand Revisited.

14: Holles Street Hospital.

15: Nighttown, Railway Street.

16: Cabman's Shelter, Custom House Quay.

17: Home, No. 7 Eccles Street.

18: Molly's Bed, No. 7 Eccles Street.

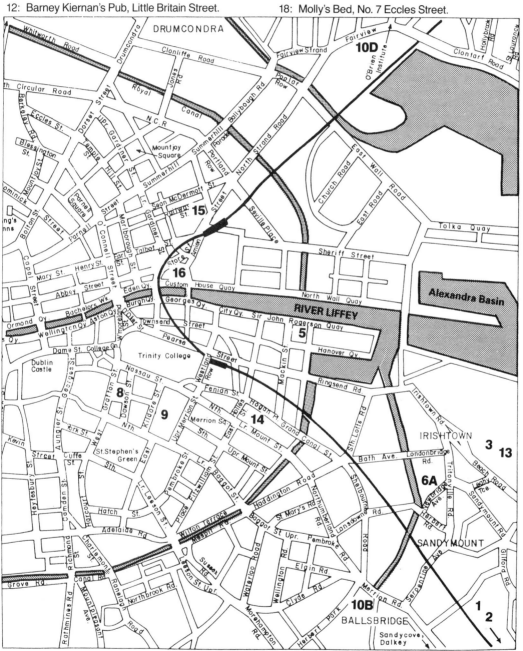

Martello Tower, Sandycove
8.00 a.m. to 8.45 a.m.
(*Chapter 1: Telemachus*)

Ulysses opens in the **Martello Tower** that stands on the shore of Dublin Bay in Sandycove Harbour, approximately seven miles southeast of the centre of Dublin. The time is 8.00 a.m., Thursday, 16 June 1904. Martello towers took their name from a fort on Cape Mortella, Corsica, whose strength had impressed the British navy during a siege in 1794. The British government erected towers on the Irish coast from 1804 to 1815 to repel a threatened invasion from France. By 1904, their military usefulness had long passed, so the British government leased them for residential and commercial uses. The one singled out in Joyce's novel is about forty feet high with walls eight feet thick. The original entrance was some ten feet off the ground.

In this first episode of *Ulysses*, Stephen Dedalus, a moody, brooding twenty-two-year-old poet and part-time teacher at a boys' school, and Buck Mulligan, a brash medical school student, are the tower's two tenants. An Englishman, Haines, is visiting them and wants to use Stephen as part of his study of Irish culture – which Stephen refuses to allow unless he is paid. This strange, Bohemian residence was a 1904 Dublin equivalent to a hippie commune of the late 1960s – an intellectual centre and a counter-culture haven from the supposed conformity and blandness of traditional living arrangements. Joyce himself spent September 9th through 14th in 1904 at this same tower with his sometime drinking buddy, Oliver St John Gogarty (1878-1957), the model for Buck Mulligan, and another guest, Samuel (later Dermot) Chenevix Trench, the model for Haines. During the night of September 14th, Trench had a nightmare and fired a revolver shot that almost hit Joyce, who left immediately never to return. Trench's life ended five years later when he shot himself in the head, perhaps with the same gun.

At the start of *Ulysses*, Buck Mulligan is shaving on the gun platform at the top of the tower and mocking the ritual of the Roman Catholic Mass. Stephen Dedalus joins him, obviously troubled. Mulligan borrows Stephen's handkerchief, remarking that he has found a 'new art colour for

TELEMACHUS

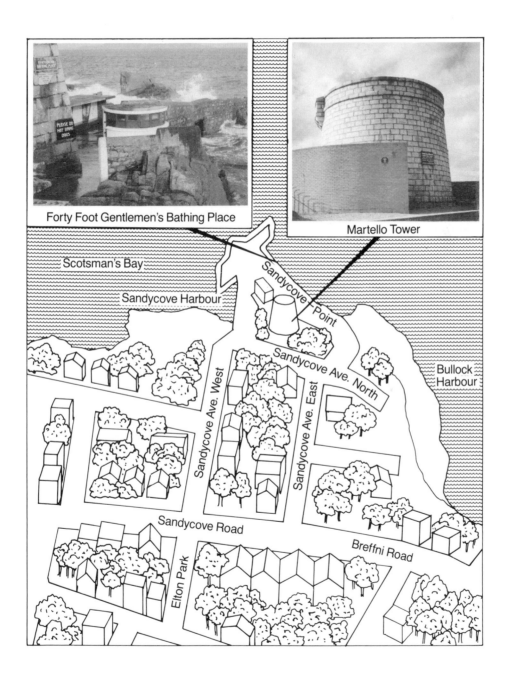

Forty Foot Gentlemen's Bathing Place

Martello Tower

Scotsman's Bay

Sandycove Harbour

Sandycove Point

Sandycove Ave. West

Sandycove Ave. North

Sandycove Ave. East

Bullock Harbour

Sandycove Road

Elton Park

Breffni Road

our Irish poets: snotgreen' (1:73). [Note: Episode (chapter) and line references for quotations from *Ulysses* are based on the corrected text edited by Hans Walter Gabler *et al.* and published by, among others, Penguin Books (Student Edition), Vintage Books in New York and Bodley Head, Ltd., in London.] The two go downstairs to a room in the tower and have breakfast with Haines, who speaks in Irish to an old milkwoman making her rounds. Soon the three young men depart – Mulligan to take a morning swim in the **Forty Foot Gentlemen's Bathing Place** a few yards away; Haines to sit on a stone and smoke; and Stephen to walk to the Summerfield Lodge School about a mile away.

The illustration on page 11 shows the location of the Martello Tower at Sandycove and the Forty Foot Gentlemen's Bathing Place. Today this tower is preserved as the **James Joyce Museum**, with some alterations from 1904. For example, Joyce had gained access to the tower by an exterior staircase, but this was removed during the remodelling and expansion of the ground floor into a museum. The breakfast room mentioned in *Ulysses* and the gun platform are essentially unchanged from 1904; the former is used as a lecture or reception room. Men (and occasionally women) still swim at the nearby bathing spot, with and without bathing suits.

Train at Seapoint circa 1904.

How to get there: DART train to Sandycove or Glenageary station and walk 15 minutes. Or take a No. 8 (Dalkey) bus from Eden Quay to Sandycove Avenue East or Breffni Road stop.

Sandycove circa 1904 (Martello Tower in distance).

OPEN DAILY FOR LADIES & GENTLEMEN

SANDYCOVE · Co.DUBLIN · 2917. W.L.

MR DEASY'S SCHOOL, DALKEY
9.40 a.m. to 10.05 a.m.
(Chapter 2: Nestor)

This chapter takes place entirely at the Summerfield Lodge School in Dalkey, a small town approximately one mile southeast of the Martello Tower at Sandycove. Stephen is teaching maths, history and English to a class of boys and tries to entertain them by asking, 'What is a pier?' His answer: 'A disappointed bridge' (2:39). After class, he receives his month's pay from the school's proprietor, Mr Deasy, who asks him to take a letter about foot-and-mouth disease in cattle to the editors of two Dublin newspapers.

Once the private residence of an Irish poet, Denis Florence McCarthy, the 1904 Summerfield Lodge housed a boys' school called the Clifton School. Joyce taught part-time there for a few weeks early that year. The founder and headmaster at the school was an Ulsterman, Francis Irwin, the prototype for Mr Deasy. Much of this chapter is based upon Joyce's recollections of his days teaching at Mr Irwin's school.

The map on the opposite page shows the probable path that Stephen took in walking from the Martello Tower in Sandycove to Mr Deasy's school in Dalkey. Stephen leaves the Martello Tower at approximately 8.45 a.m. and walks to Summerfield Lodge, probably along Sandycove Avenue East, Breffni Road, Ulverton Road and Dalkey Avenue. A private residence again, Summerfield Lodge still stands at 63 Dalkey Avenue with its large lawns – on which the boys played field hockey – intact. A visitor can still see the gate pillars, now without lions, where Mr Deasy observed (quite incorrectly) to Stephen that 'Ireland . . . has the honour of being the only country which never persecuted the jews . . . And do you know why? . . . Because she never let them in' (2:437-42).

How to get there: DART train to Dalkey station and walk through Dalkey village. Or take a No. 8 bus (Dalkey) from Eden Quay to Dalkey village stop.

NESTOR

••• Stephen's Probable Route
(Not Actually Taken During This Chapter)

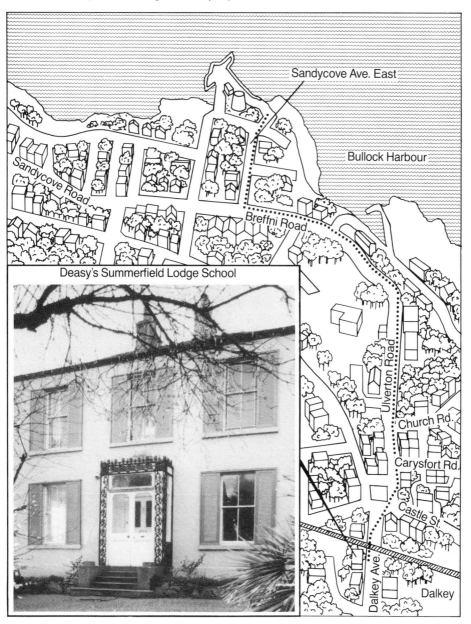

Sandycove Ave. East

Bullock Harbour

Sandycove Road

Breffni Road

Deasy's Summerfield Lodge School

Ulverton Road

Church Rd.

Carysfort Rd.

Castle St.

Dalkey Ave.

Dalkey

SANDYMOUNT STRAND
11.00 a.m. to 11.30 a.m.
(Chapter 3: Proteus)

The scene of this chapter is **Sandymount Strand**, a beach just south of the Liffey River and approximately five miles north from the Martello Tower in Sandycove. For about thirty minutes Stephen, deep in thought, walks along this beach.

A Joyce enthusiast today who wants to trace Stephen's exact footsteps in the sand will be sadly disappointed. As the maps on page 19 indicate, the Sandymount Strand on which Stephen walked into eternity no longer exists. Danis Rose, a Joyce scholar residing in the Strawberry Beds (18:948) just outside Dublin, has argued that Stephen's path followed the route as indicated on the top map on page 19. Today the former beach area has been filled in and is now the site of a school, roads, houses and a sports grounds as shown on the lower map on page 19.

While unable to follow Stephen's precise journey, a visitor today may still get the taste of this chapter by walking along the existing Sandymount Strand. Tide permitting, you may stroll along the beach from Marine Drive to another Martello tower at St John's Road. You can still hear the 'crush, crack, crick, crick' (3:19) of shells and see the **Pigeonhouse** (3:160) electrical generating station of Joyce's day (it's now the middle building with the shortest chimney stack) as well as the waves or 'whitemaned seahorses' (3:56). The sight of the Pigeonhouse reminds Stephen of an irreverent French joke about the Holy Family, which can be translated as: 'Who has put you in this wretched condition? It was the pigeon, Joseph' (3:161-162).

The map on page 17 shows Stephen's probable journey from Dalkey to Sandymount Strand. In all likelihood he took the train at the Dalkey station, got off at Lansdowne Road, walked over the bridge at the Dodder River, took a left onto Newbridge Avenue, crossed Tritonville Road and went down Leahy's Terrace to the beach, in part following the route that Bloom takes to get to Sandymount Strand in chapter 13. (In the spring of 1904, when Joyce himself worked at Mr. Irwin's school in Dalkey, he lived

PROTEUS

··· Stephen's Probable Train Route
(Not Actually Taken During This Chapter)

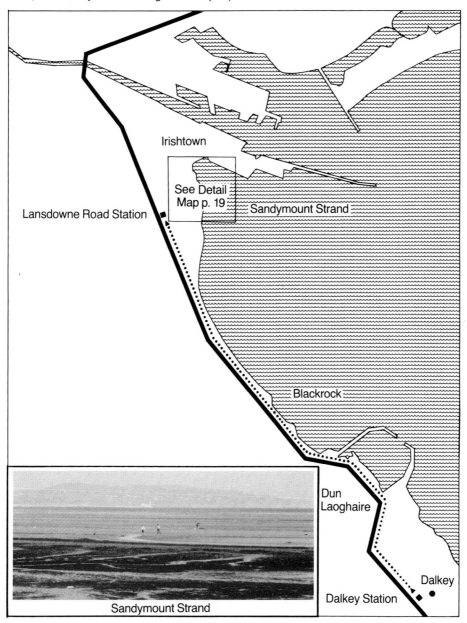

Irishtown

See Detail
Map p. 19

Lansdowne Road Station

Sandymount Strand

Blackrock

Dun
Laoghaire

Dalkey

Dalkey Station

Sandymount Strand

at **No. 60 Shelbourne Road**, just around the corner from Lansdowne Road Station; thus, in heading off for work in the morning, he would have taken the train to Dalkey, and, when he felt like a stroll on the beach, he would have taken the same route that Stephen does in this chapter.) Stephen has some extra time prior to a scheduled meeting with Buck Mulligan at 12.30 p.m. at a pub called The Ship at No. 5 Lower Abbey Street in the centre of Dublin (a meeting Stephen later decides to avoid). He thinks about paying a call to the house of his uncle, Richie Goulding, in **Strasburg Terrace**, Irishtown, but apparently never makes that visit.

Today, a Joycean can take the DART train from Dalkey, get off at the Lansdowne Road stop (near Lansdowne Rugby Ground, Ireland's largest rugby stadium) and follow Stephen's path down Leahy's Terrace (albeit finding a school and road where Stephen found beach).

It is unclear whether Stephen walks or takes a tram to the newspaper office in the centre of Dublin, where he is next seen some time after noon. He does stop at the College Green post office to send a telegram to Buck Mulligan at The Ship, cancelling the meeting. Stephen is heading towards the centre of Dublin at approximately the same time that Leopold Bloom is travelling in the same direction with the funeral cortège (see chapter 6).

How to get there: DART train to Lansdowne Road station. Or take a No. 2 or 3 (Sandymount) bus from O'Connell Street to Leahy's Terrace (Star of the Sea Church) stop.

SANDYMOUNT STRAND DETAIL MAP

Sandymount Strand circa 1904
Dotted Area Indicates Beach At Low Tide

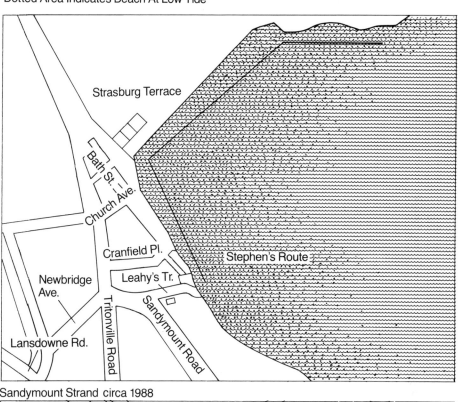

Sandymount Strand circa 1988

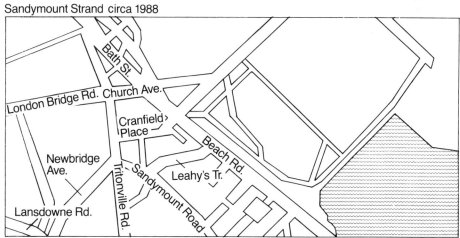

No 7 Eccles Street
8.00 a.m. to 8.45 a.m.
(*Chapter 4: Calypso*)

In this chapter *Ulysses* jumps back in time to its starting point and we meet Leopold Bloom, a thirty-eight-year-old advertising salesman for a Dublin daily newspaper, the *Freeman's Journal* (later absorbed into the *Irish Independent* newspaper group). Bloom is preparing breakfast for his thirty-three-year-old wife, Molly, an amateur opera singer soon to perform in a Belfast concert arranged by her lover, Blazes Boylan. She is still half asleep, so he walks around the corner to buy a kidney from Dlugacz's butcher shop for his own breakfast, speculating on the way that a 'good puzzle would be cross Dublin without passing a pub' (4:129-30).

The map on the opposite page shows the Blooms' house at No. 7 Eccles Street (demolished in the 1970s to make way for the **Mater Private Hospital**) and follows Bloom's path as he goes to buy the kidney. He crosses over to the opposite side of Eccles Street, turns right at Larry O'Rourke's Pub at 72-73 Upper Dorset Street (since renamed the **James Joyce Lounge**). He passes St Joseph's School (now St Raphael's House) and buys the pork kidney at Dlugacz's butcher shop (one of the few entirely imaginary stores in *Ulysses*). The chapter ends with Bloom hearing the bells of **St George's**, a nearby Protestant church (4:544-550).

Though, regrettably, one cannot now see No. 7 Eccles Street, a visitor may get an impression of Bloom's house from the Georgian townhouses on the other side of Eccles Street (especially No. 77). This area still retains the atmosphere of Joyce's Dublin. Note the magnificent iron railings around St George's Church. The door to No. 7 Eccles Street is carefully preserved at The Bailey Restaurant in Duke Street while the brick doorway is with the Irish Tourist Board and awaiting reconstruction at some suitable location.

How to get there: Take 3, 11, 11a, 22, 22a, 36 or 36a (Drumcondra) bus from Upper Dorset Street to Eccles Street stop.

CALYPSO

— Bloom's Route
■ Stopping Point

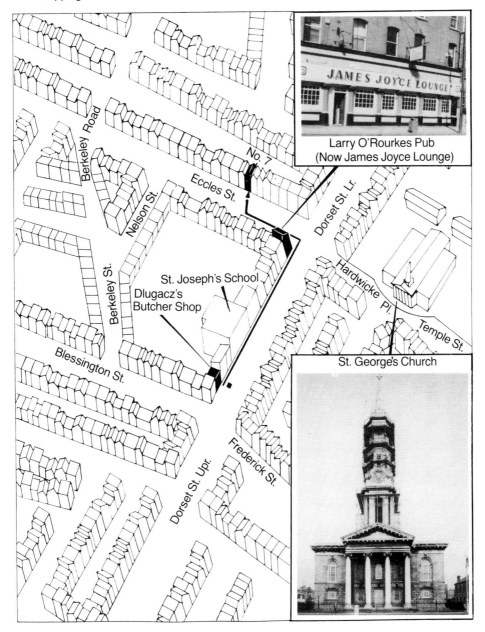

Larry O'Rourkes Pub
(Now James Joyce Lounge)

St. George's Church

Opposite: O'Connell Bridge circa 1904 with left to right statues of Smith O'Brien, O'Connell, Gray and Nelson's Pillar (see page 32).

St. George's Church circa 1904.

South Dublin Streets
9.40 a.m. to 10.05 a.m.
(Chapter 5: Lotus Eaters)

In this chapter Bloom walks along the Liffey River and through a commercial district of Dublin, making three main stops: first at a post office to pick up a letter, second at the **St Andrew's** (which Joyce calls All Hallows) **Roman Catholic Church**, and third at **Sweny's Chemist's Shop** (pharmacy).

Bloom's path from the Liffey to the **Westland Row Post Office** traces a question mark. It is clearly not the shortest path he could have taken. He may want to avoid being seen going to the post office to pick up a letter from a female admirer or perhaps he is just wandering aimlessly. In any case, he is first seen heading east along **'sir John Rogerson's Quay'** (5:1), a dock area across the Liffey from the **Custom House**, one of the most magnificent Georgian buildings in Dublin. Bloom turns right (south) on Lime Street, now a warehouse area with high stone walls, then takes the first right onto Hanover Street (which becomes Townsend Street). His walk along Lime and Hanover streets is only briefly mentioned in the novel. After taking a left onto Lombard Street East, he notices the Bethel Salvation Army Hall (5:10-11) and the offices of **'Nichols' the undertaker'** (5:11) – which are still at Nos. 26-31. He crosses Great Brunswick Street (now Pearse Street) and walks along Westland Row past the old Grosvenor Hotel, pausing in front of the Belfast and Oriental Tea Company storefront under the train tracks. Bloom then crosses the street to pick up a letter at the Westland Row Post Office from a Martha Clifford. He had been secretly corresponding with her under the alias of Henry Flower. Today, only the brick facade of the post office remains; it is now part of the Westland Row train station.

Bloom's route from the post office to **St Andrew's (All Hallows)** is also in the shape of a question mark. Upon leaving the post office, he turns to the right and retraces his steps back down Westland Row. He meets an acquaintance named M'Coy and tries to '[g]et rid of him quickly' (5:82). He turns right on Brunswick (Pearse) Street and takes another right onto Cumberland Street, where he pauses. The secluded area next to the

LOTUS EATERS

■ Bloom's Route   ••• Projected Route
■ Stopping Points

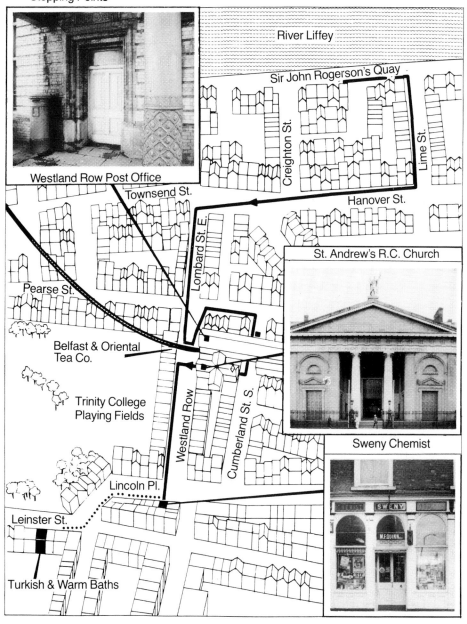

Westland Row Post Office

River Liffey

Sir John Rogerson's Quay

Creighton St.

Lime St.

Townsend St.

Hanover St.

Lombard St. E.

Pearse St.

St. Andrew's R.C. Church

Belfast & Oriental Tea Co.

Trinity College Playing Fields

Westland Row

Cumberland St. S.

Sweny Chemist

Lincoln Pl.

Leinster St.

Turkish & Warm Baths

'station wall' (5:230), still today a dark, cavernous, somewhat sinister place, provides a perfect spot to read Martha's letter in private. Bloom then goes under the railway tracks and tears the envelope 'swiftly in shreds' (5:300-301). Continuing for a few steps in the same direction, he takes a right into the back entrance of All Hallows, where he watches Mass from the Communion to the end of the service. You should note that the 'open backdoor' (5:318) of the church is now usually locked, except for daily and Sunday masses. The visitor may still attend morning mass at 10.00 a.m. (a little later than Bloom) and see the 'confessionbox' (5:366), the magnificent organ in the choir (5:395), and the marble holy water bowl on the front steps (5:458).

Bloom takes a more direct path to his third stop in the chapter – **Sweny's Chemist's Shop**. Leaving All Hallows by the main entrance, he makes a left turn onto Westland Row. At the intersection of Westland Row and Lincoln Place, he crosses the road and enters Sweny's, where he orders some skin lotion for Molly and buys lemon soap for fourpence. Though prominently displaying the name of the new owner, M. F. Quinn, on the storefront, the shop in Lincoln Place also still keeps the name Sweny, as a conspicuous tribute to the Joyce industry. 'Chemists rarely move,' Bloom correctly predicted (5:463-464). Sweny's still stocks lemon soap (though not the brand it carried in 1904). The chapter ends with Bloom thinking about taking a bath as he walks towards the 'oriental edifice of the Turkish and Warm Baths, 11 Leinster Street' (17:338-339). This 'mosque of the baths' (5:549) has not survived.

How to get there: See index map. Within walking distance of O'Connell Street.

Sir John Rogerson's Quay.

St. Andrew's Church, Westland Row.

Nichols'.

Westland Row Post Office.

Secluded area near station wall.

Back of All Hallows.

Funeral Procession Across Dublin
11.00 a.m. to 11.45 a.m.
(*Chapter 6: Hades*)

In this episode Bloom travels with the funeral procession accompanying the body of Paddy Dignam (who died from a stroke). The journey starts from the Dignam house in Sandymount and ends at **Glasnevin Cemetery**, where such Irish patriots as Daniel O'Connell and Charles Stewart Parnell are buried. This chapter contains the longest single journey of main characters in *Ulysses*, a trek of about four miles. Bloom rides in a horse-drawn carriage with Stephen's father (Simon Dedalus), Martin Cunningham and Jack Power. At Glasnevin Cemetery, Bloom attends the service in the chapel and follows the mourners to the graveside. All then return to the centre of Dublin. While many chapters of *Ulysses* show characters walking through Dublin, this episode constitutes one of the few instances in which the trip is made on wheels. Perhaps only hardy Joyceans should try to walk it today.

The map on the opposite page shows the route of the funeral procession. The funeral cortège starts at **No. 9 Newbridge Avenue** in Sandymount and takes an initial route roughly parallel to the shore of Dublin Bay. One of the passengers, Martin Cunningham, outlines the first part of the journey – 'Irishtown . . . Ringsend. Brunswick street' (6:34). 'That's a fine old custom' (6:36), Mr. Dedalus says, referring to the practice of passersby doffing their hats to the hearse. The carriage goes north on Tritonville Road into Irishtown Road and then on into Thomas Street. The carriage turns west (left) *via* Fitzwilliam Street (where Ringsend Library is now located) onto Bridge Street which becomes, first, Ringsend Road and then Great Brunswick Street (now Pearse Street) – all heading towards the centre of Dublin. After going down the short D'Olier Street onto Sackville Street (now O'Connell Street) across the River Liffey, the procession then goes by way of Parnell Square, Frederick Street, Blessington Street, Berkeley Street, North Circular Road, Phibsborough Road, Prospect Road and Finglas Road, to arrive at **Glasnevin Cemetery**.

The passengers in the carriage see a number of Dublin places and

HADES

—— Route of the Funeral Cortege
★ Sees Stephen

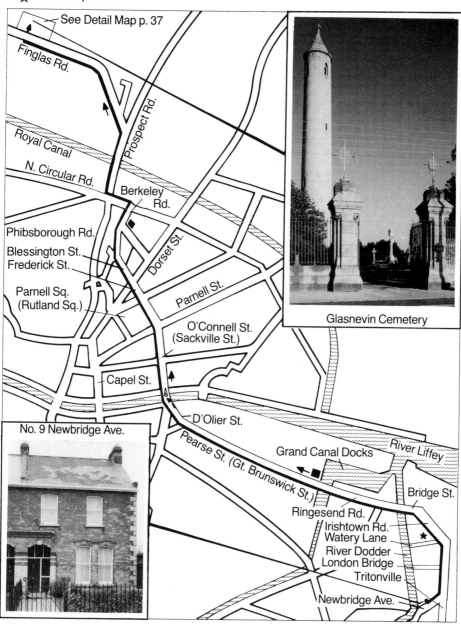

See Detail Map p. 37

Finglas Rd.

Prospect Rd.

Royal Canal

N. Circular Rd.

Berkeley Rd.

Phibsborough Rd.

Blessington St.
Frederick St.

Dorset St.

Parnell Sq.
(Rutland Sq.)

Parnell St.

O'Connell St.
(Sackville St.)

Glasnevin Cemetery

Capel St.

D'Olier St.

No. 9 Newbridge Ave.

Pearse St. (Gt. Brunswick St.)

Grand Canal Docks

River Liffey

Bridge St.

Ringesend Rd.

Irishtown Rd.
Watery Lane

River Dodder
London Bridge

Tritonville

Newbridge Ave.

people. They cross water four times: the Dodder, the Grand Canal, the Liffey and the Royal Canal, representing the four rivers of hell. Bloom sees Stephen – for the first time that day – after they pass Watery Lane (now Dermot O'Hurley Avenue) in Irishtown; 'clad in mourning, a wide hat' (6:39). Stephen's mother had died in Dublin in June 1903 (Joyce's mother had died in August 1903), and 'both' were buried in Glasnevin. The entourage is stopped momentarily by the swing bridge over the Grand Canal to let a barge through. They pass the 'gasworks', a foul-smelling plant in which coal was turned into gas. Recalling the old Dublin custom of bringing children with chest complaints there to sniff the air, Bloom thinks 'Whooping cough they say it cures' (6:121). After the party passes the Antient Concert Rooms (6:180), now housing the **Academy** theatre and various shops, at 42 Great Brunswick Street (now Pearse Street) – where Joyce sang with Ireland's most famous tenor, John MacCormack, on August 27, 1904 – Bloom boasts that his wife Molly will soon do a concert in Belfast with 'all topnobbers. J. C. Doyle and John MacCormack . . . [t]he best in fact' (6:221-223). The carriage goes down D'Olier Street (where Blazes Boylan has his offices, probably at number 15) and passes the statue of William Smith O'Brien (6:226), a leader of the 1848 rising who died on June 16, 1864 (the statue has since been moved from the junction of D'Olier and Westmoreland Streets north to O'Connell Street), and next 'the hugecloaked Liberator's form' (6:249), the twelve-foot, **bronze statue of Irish patriot Daniel O'Connell** (1775-1847), still wrapped in his cloak atop a twenty-eight foot pedestal. Other memorials that they pass are, in order: **Sir John Gray's statue**, Nelson's Pillar (blown up in 1966), **Father Mathew's statue** and the foundation stone for **Parnell's monument** (since completed). Many of the buildings along Sackville Street (now O'Connell Street) were destroyed in the 1916 Rising and the 1922 Civil War. Of the commercial tenants along O'Connell Street mentioned by Bloom, only the building at No. 42 is still standing. In 1904 it housed the 'catholic club' (6:318); today it is empty and awaiting reconstruction, although the Royal Dublin Hotel uses a main room of the old building for receptions.

The procession passes the 'Rotunda corner' (6:321-322), a series of buildings at the intersection of Sackville Street Upper and Cavendish Road (now Parnell Street), originally opened in 1757 as a maternity hospital and expanded to include assembly halls. Today, the assembly halls house the Gate Theatre and a cinema; unfortunately, the billboards advertising the current movie often hide much of this magnificent 18th century building. The carriage then goes onto Frederick Street *via* Rutland Square (now Parnell Square), then to Blessington Street and Berkeley Street (6:372). Any Joycean today trying to drive the funeral cortège route will find that Frederick and Blessington Streets are now one-way streets going

Rotunda circa 1904.

the wrong way. Bloom and the others pass the **Mater Misericordiae** (6:375) – the largest hospital in Dublin at the time – at the intersection of Berkeley Road (the continuation of Berkeley Street) and Eccles Street, where Bloom lives. The procession turns left (west) onto the North Circular Road, then right at Dunphy's Corner onto Phibsborough Road. Dunphy's Corner was named for a well-known pub operated by Thomas Dunphy until about 1890 at 160-161 Phibsborough Road. In 1904 the pub was run by John Doyle, and over the following years the name of the corner was changed to **Doyle's Corner**. Today the pub is named (after a 'literary' relative) the **Sir Arthur Conan Doyle**. Long-time residents of that area still recall when Dunphy's (or Doyle's) pub was a famous stop after a burial at Glasnevin Cemetery.

The entourage crosses the **Royal Canal** (6:438) – which Joyce describes in terms suggestive of the mythical River Styx – over the **Cross Guns Bridge** (a pub at the bridge is still called the Cross Guns). Just to the north of the bridge they pass '**Brian Boroimhe house**' (6:453), a pub named for Brian Boru at No. 1 Prospect Terrace on the corner of Prospect Road. Brian Boru, Ireland's most famous king, was killed in a victory over the Danes at Clontarf (about a mile east of the pub) in 1014. This pub still exists today; the Hedigan family has owned the business since November 1904 and the building has been there since about 1850. Finally, the carriage turns left onto Finglas Road, the southern boundary of **Glasnevin Cemetery**. Thos. H. Dennany's (6:462) display of cemetery markers was just off Finglas Road on Prospect Avenue. It is no longer there (on the site today is a flower shop), but nearby is another tombstone shop. The house where 'childs was murdered' (6:469) was located at 5 Bengal Terrace. Samuel Childs was tried (and acquitted) for the murder of his seventy-six-year-old brother at that house near Glasnevin Cemetery.

You can still see today the 'dark poplars' and 'high railings of Prospect' (6:486) where the carriage stops and the mourners walk to the grave. The coffin is taken from the hearse at the gates of the cemetery and carried through the gates, followed by the mourners. The party turns to the left towards '**the cardinal's mausoleum**' (6:534), and then into the mortuary chapel to the right. The mausoleum, erected in 1887, is to Cardinal McCabe. (Today, there is a second mausoleum: to Archbishop Walsh.) After the service, the coffin is carried out the side door on the right of the chapel and down a gravel path to the left (6:637). To the right of the path is Daniel O'Connell's crypt (6:641-642) and to the left, further on, is the grave of Stephen's mother (6:645). After this point the text ceases to be specific: we are told that the coffin 'turned into a side lane' (6:708), but not whether this is to the left or the right. No exact location for the 'Dignam' grave is given. We do know, however, that the 'Hades' chapter is based on

34

a real funeral that took place in July 1904 which was attended by many of the people who appear as characters in *Ulysses*, including Joyce's father and Alfred H. Hunter, a model for Bloom. This was the funeral of Matthew F. Kane (17:1253), a man whose spirit haunts *Ulysses*; he was the model for Patrick Dignam, Martin Cunningham (who thereby attends his own funeral) and even, in 'Circe', William Shakespeare (whom he resembled physically). His grave is in the St. Brigid's section of the cemetery and is as good a spot as any to locate Dignam's resting place.

The map (page 37) shows the approximate positions of 'Joycean' graves referred to in the text. To find these the visitor should be aware that the cemetery is laid out, like Washington, D.C., in 'streets' (rows of graves) running east to west and named after the letters of the alphabet, and, running south to north, numbered. Thus, Matthew Kane's grave is No. Ii-238½, while Joyce's mother's is No. Xf-7. Bloom's family plot (which of course is fictional) is to the west of Kane's, 'over there towards Finglas' (6:862).

Glasnevin Cemetery is the 'Hades' of *Ulysses* in another sense also; many of the characters who inhabit its pages are buried here, as prophesied by Bloom: 'How many! All these here once walked round Dublin. Faithful departed' (6:960). Some scholar, someday, may find them all again; here are two: Michael Cusack, 'the Citizen' of 'Cyclops' (see chapter 12), rests in peace at No. Dg-163½, where his fierce, bearded visage, along with his name in Irish (Ciosog), is carved on his tomb; and Canon John O'Hanlon, the priest who officiates at the ceremony in the Star of the Sea Church in Sandymount while Bloom gazes at Gerty MacDowell in 'Nausicaa' (see chapter 13), lies under a celtic cross at No. Eh-19.

How to get there: For No. 9 Newbridge Avenue, take DART train to Lansdowne Road station or No. 2 or 3 (Sandymount) bus from O'Connell Street to Leahy's Terrace (Star of the Sea Church) stop. For Glasnevin Cemetery take No. 35, 40a, 40b, 40c (Finglas) bus from intersection of Parnell Street and Parnell Square East to Prospect Cemetery on Finglas Road.

Side door of the Chapel and the Gravel Path, lined with Dark Poplars.

GLASNEVIN CEMETERY DETAIL MAP

---Projected Route of Mourners

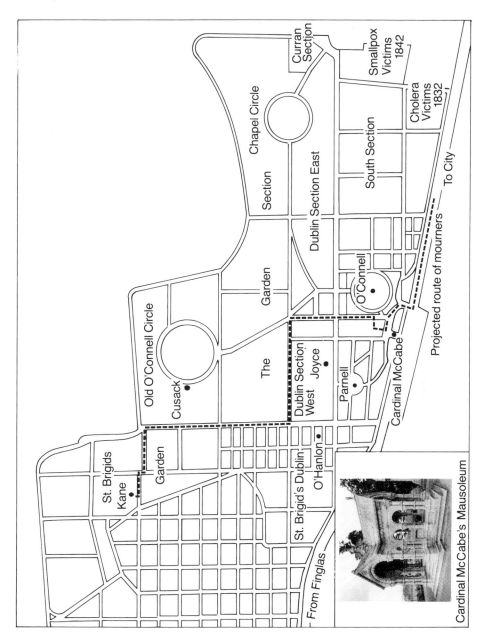

Citizen's Tomb (note his portrait).

The grave of Joyce's parents.

THE FREEMAN'S JOURNAL
12.00 noon to 1.00 p.m.
(*Chapter 7: Aeolus*)

This chapter takes place for the most part at the former offices of the *Freeman's Journal* and *Evening Telegraph* (absorbed into the *Irish Independent* in about 1925) at 4-8 Prince's Street North. Located just off O'Connell Street, the newspaper office building ran through from Prince's Street to Abbey Street. This is another of the chapters in which Stephen and Bloom cross paths but do not meet. In 1904, the population of Dublin was less than 300,000 (today it is over 1,000,000), and Dubliners often bumped into one another quite by chance on the streets and in shops and offices. At about noon Bloom visits the editors of the *Freeman's Journal* to discuss the renewal of an advertisement for Alexander Keyes, wine merchant. At the same time, Stephen Dedalus, fulfilling his promise, is presenting to the paper a copy of the letter from Mr Deasy on foot-and-mouth disease in cattle.

The illustration opposite shows the former location of the newspaper offices, a site now occupied by British Home Stores, and the routes taken by various characters in this chapter. Bloom enters the newspaper building via the printing rooms on Prince's Street, leaves via Abbey Street and walks down William's Row (now Bachelor's Way) to speak to Mr Keyes at Dillon's Auction Rooms on Bachelor's Walk, and, disappointed, returns to the newspaper office. He then departs for the National Library to look for a copy of the *Kilkenny People* carrying the Keyes advertisement. Also shown are the paths taken to pubs: by Simon Dedalus and his friend to the **Oval** and by Stephen Dedalus and others across O'Connell Street to **Mooney's** (now called the Abbey Mooney). The exterior of the Oval looks much the same today; Mooney's exterior has been extensively remodelled. Both serve frothy Guinness stout and other beverages to quench the thirst of footsore peripatetic Joyceans.

How to get there: See location on index map. Within walking distance of O'Connell Street.

AEOLUS

━━━━ Route Of Stephen and Others --- Bloom's Route
•••••• Route Of Simon Dedalus

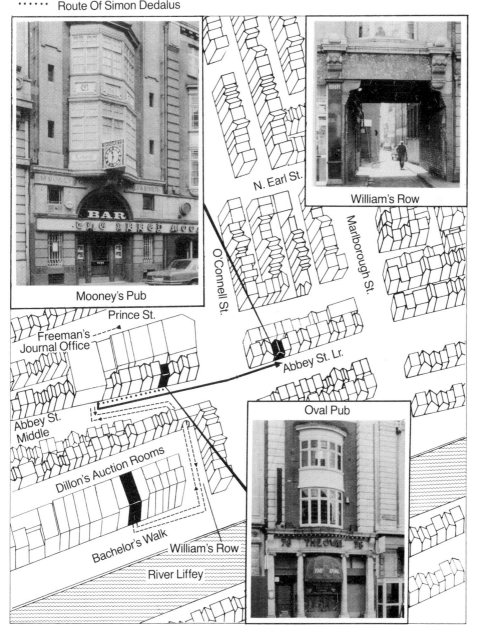

Mooney's Pub

William's Row

N. Earl St.

O'Connell St.

Marlborough St.

Prince St.

Freeman's Journal Office

Abbey St. Lr.

Oval Pub

Abbey St. Middle

Dillon's Auction Rooms

Bachelor's Walk

William's Row

River Liffey

LUNCH AT DAVY BYRNE'S
1.00 a.m. to 2.00 p.m.
(*Chapter 8: Lestrygonians*)

This chapter covers Bloom's walk from the offices of the *Freeman's Journal* to the **National Museum**. He travels south across the River Liffey (stopping on the bridge to throw two Banbury cakes to the birds) and has lunch at that most famous Joycean pub, **Davy Byrne's**, which is still serving excellent food (try the smoked salmon) and drink at 21 Duke Street. Much of the chapter is about Bloom's observations and thoughts on a variety of subjects, especially food.

Bloom's route is shown on the opposite page. It starts at O'Connell Street (then called Sackville Street). He walks south, passing Lemon and Company, Ltd., a candy shop and small factory that was then located at No. 49, and reads or recalls their advertisement 'Lozenge and comfit manufacturer to His Majesty the King', picturing his highness 'on his throne sucking red jujubes white' (8:3-4). Look closely at the Old Bridge Restaurant building and see the name (now somewhat faded) 'The Confectioners Hall' remaining from the days of Lemon's sweet shop. Bloom also looks down Bachelor's Walk to the right where he notices Stephen's destitute sister 'selling off some old furniture' (8:29) at Dillon's Auction Rooms, then at No. 25 (today a snooker hall). While crossing over O'Connell Bridge, he throws two Banbury cakes to the seagulls in the Liffey (8:74-76). On the south side of the Liffey, Bloom 'smile[s]' at two windows of the **Ballast Office** (8:114), at the corner of Westmoreland Street and Aston Quay, which housed the offices of the Dublin Port and Docks Board in 1904. The Ballast Office building has been completely rebuilt – the 'timeball' is no more and the clock is now on the Liffey side instead of the Westmoreland Street side of the building as it was in 1904. He crosses Westmoreland Street (8:155) and meets Mrs. Breen, an old acquaintance, outside 'Harrison's' Confectioners (8:233), 29 Westmoreland Street, now the Dublin Pharmacy (an optician despite the name).

Continuing, Bloom walks by *The Irish Times* office at 31 Westmoreland Street (now occupied by the Educational Building Society), recalling the

LESTRYGONIANS

— Bloom's Route
■ Stopping Points

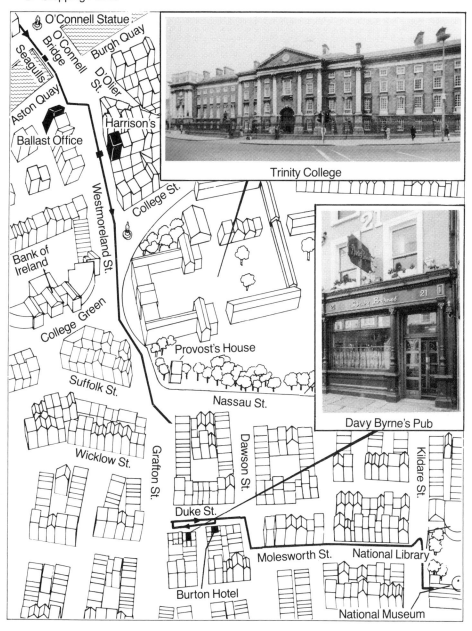

O'Connell Statue
O'Connell Bridge
Burgh Quay
D'Olier St.
Seagulls
Aston Quay
Harrison's
Ballast Office
Westmoreland St.
College St.

Trinity College

Bank of Ireland
College Green
Suffolk St.
Provost's House
Nassau St.

Davy Byrne's Pub

Wicklow St.
Grafton St.
Dawson St.
Kildare St.
Duke St.
Molesworth St.
National Library
Burton Hotel
National Museum

43

advertisement he placed that brought him into contact with Martha Clifford: 'Wanted, smart lady typist to aid gentleman in literary work' (8:326-327). Near the 'Irish house of parliament' (8:401) Bloom speculates on what the pigeons above might be saying: 'Who will we do it on? I pick the fellow in black' (8:402-403). **The Bank of Ireland** building housed the Irish Parliament until Great Britain dissolved it by the Act of Union in 1800. Next, Bloom 'crossed under Tommy Moore's roguish finger' (8:414) – a statue, still standing, of the Irish poet, songwriter and musician, Thomas Moore (1779-1852). Bloom thinks: 'They did right to put him up over a urinal: meeting of the waters' (8:414-415), a common Dublin joke and a reference to his poem 'The Meeting of the Waters' in *Moore's Irish Melodies*.

Seeing **Trinity College**, Bloom recalls the young students who protested against British Prime Minister Joseph Chamberlain receiving an honorary degree in 1899 with a comment equally relevant to the student protestors of 1968-71: 'Few years' time half of them magistrates and civil servants' (8:438-439). He then passes 'Trinity's surly front' (8:476), the massive stone facade of the university shown in the picture on page 43. Next on Bloom's route are the **'Provost's house'** (8:496), still the home of the Provost of Trinity College and one of the most splendid private residences in Dublin, and 'Walter Sexton's window' (8:500) across the street from the provost's house (Walter Sexton, goldsmith, jeweller, silversmith and watchmaker at 118 Grafton Street, a site now occupied by a Thomas Cook Travel Agency). In front of the window of Yeates and Sons (which stood at the corner of Grafton and Nassau streets until the 1970s) Bloom pauses, 'pricing the fieldglasses' (8:552). After passing La Maison Claire (a court milliner and dressmaker formerly at 4 Grafton Street) and Adam Court, a tiny passageway still off Grafton Street, Bloom notes his surroundings: 'gay with housed awnings [they] lured his senses' (8:614). Then, as today, Grafton Street was a fashionable Dublin shopping district. He passes, 'dallying, the windows of **Brown Thomas**, silk mercers' (8:620). Brown Thomas remains one of Dublin's most elegant department stores.

Bloom's next wandering in this chapter takes him to Duke Street (off Grafton Street) in search of something to eat. He turns at Combridge's Corner (Combridge and Co., picture-frame makers, then at the intersection of Grafton Street with Duke Street – now part of Brown Thomas, while Combridge's has moved to Suffolk Street). He first stops in the Burton (formally known as the Burton Hotel and Billiard Rooms, at 18 Duke Street), where the sight of the lunch crowd disgusts him: 'Stink gripped his trembling breath: pungent meatjuice, slush of greens. See the animals feed' (8:650-652). Leaving the Burton, Bloom backtracks three shopfronts to **Davy Byrne's** at 21 Duke Street, which for many years bore on its sign Bloom's description of it: 'Moral pub' (8:732). Bloom recalls Davy Byrne: 'He doesn't chat. Stands a drink now and then. But in leapyear once in four' (8:732-733). For lunch, while chatting with Nosey Flynn, whose mouth is so wide he 'could whistle in his own ear' (8:768) Bloom has a glass of burgundy and a Gorgonzola cheese sandwich with mustard . Davy Byrne's was extensively expanded and remodelled in 1942 in an art deco style with wall murals by Cecil ffrench Salkeld, Brendan Behan's father-in-law. There is a painting there of Joyce by Harry Kernoff and another by William Orpen showing Davy Byrne himself.

After lunch, Bloom leaves Davy Byrne's, turning right towards Dawson Street and passing Duke Lane and 'William Miller, plumber' at 17 Duke Street (8:1045). Walking further, he looks across the street at John Long's, a pub at 52 Dawson Street on the corner of Duke Street – now a delicatessen called Graham O'Sullivan – then turns right (south) onto Dawson Street near 'Gray's confectioner's window' (8:10969), 13 Duke Street, a site now occupied by a newsagent. He passes the Rev. Thomas Connellan's Bookstore at 51B Dawson Street, an establishment specializing in protestant evangelical tracts (the site now houses a cake shop called the Tea Time Express, and one can still see the display window once used for books). The sight of a bakery and a religious bookstore reminds Bloom of the connection between food and religion: 'They say they used to give pauper children soup to change to protestants in the time of the potato blight' (8:1071-1073). Bloom helps a blind youth across Dawson Street and passes Drago's (Adolphe Drago, Parisian perfumer and hairdresser, at 17 Dawson Street), the Stewart Institution for Imbecile Children at 40 Molesworth Street and Doran's Pub at 10 Molesworth Street – all of these buildings have since been demolished and the area extensively redeveloped. The map on page 43 shows how bloom changes direction when, continuing into Kildare Street, he turns left to enter the **National Library**, but then catches sight of Blazes Boylan, Molly's current lover. To avoid meeting Boylan, Bloom veers away from the National Library and heads instead for the **National Museum**. The chapter ends with Bloom looking at the statues known as the Goddesses, which used to stand in the round foyer inside the National Museum before they were removed in the 1920s.

How to get there: See location on index map. Within walking distance of O'Connell Street.

45

Trinity College circa 1904.

Intersection of Nassau Street and Grafton Street circa 1904.

Grafton Street circa 1904.

THE NATIONAL LIBRARY
2.00 p.m. to 2.45 p.m.
(Chapter 9: Scylla and Charybdis)

In this chapter, Stephen, the bookman *par excellence*, is seen in a room at the **National Library**, Kildare Street, talking about his interpretation of *Hamlet*, which he offers for a guinea, with some very distinguished Dubliners: AE (George Russell), the writer; W. K. Magee, also a writer, who used the nom de plume 'John Eglinton'; Thomas Lyster, the Quaker librarian; and the assistant librarian, R. I. Best, an accomplished Celtic scholar. Mulligan, who has come from the Ship tavern in search of Haines, arrives in the middle of Stephen's discourse. Bloom also enters the library, once again crossing paths with Stephen without meeting. While the discussion about *Hamlet* is going on, Bloom copies the advertisement he needs from the *Kilkenny People*. Stephen and Mulligan leave the library about 2.45 p.m., passing Bloom near the 'portico' of the library (9:1205).

The **National Library** has great historical significance for the Irish literary movement. Joyce may well have rejected the direction of the movement, but every Irish writer and scholar of distinction – George Bernard Shaw, Oscar Wilde, W. B. Yeats, and John Millington Synge – walked and talked on the steps of the library. The magnificent, domed building looks much like it did in 1904. The steps, porch, pillars and exterior facade are practically the same. Only the gates and fencing have been altered, for security reasons, since the adjacent building, Leinster House, is now the seat of the Irish Parliament. A visitor must still go to the reference (inquiry) desk where Bloom asked to see the files of the *Kilkenny People* for 1903 (9:586-587). The room where the discussion of *Hamlet* took place is now the office in which visitors apply for readers' tickets and for photocopying. On the stair landing you can see a plaque to Thomas Lyster, the Quaker librarian.

How to get there: Within walking distance of O'Connell Street. Or take No. 10 (Belfield), No. 11 (Clonskea), No. 14 (Churchtown) or No. 20, 20b (Bulfin Road) bus from O'Connell Street to Kildare Street, Leinster House stop.

SCYLLA AND CHARYBDIS

—— Stephen and Buck Mulligan
■ Pass Bloom At Portico

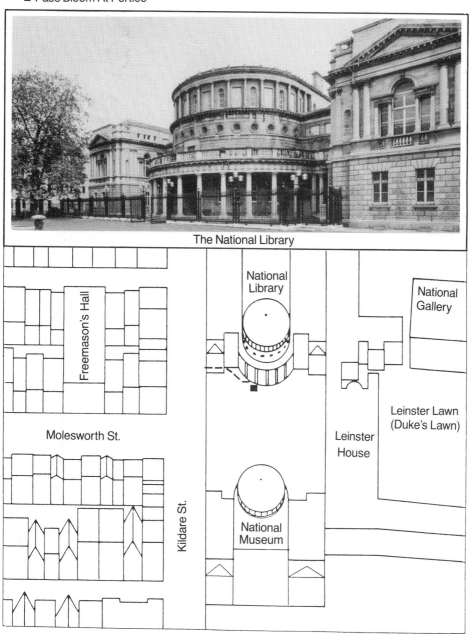

The National Library

National Library

National Gallery

Freemason's Hall

Molesworth St.

Kildare St.

National Museum

Leinster House

Leinster Lawn (Duke's Lawn)

National Library (left) and Leinster House circa 1904.

Reading Room of the National Library circa 1904.

T. W. Lyster, Librarian 1895-1920. This room is where the discussion on *Hamlet* took place. Note portrait engraving of Shakespeare on left.

CITY ODYSSEY
2.55 p.m. to 4.00 p.m.
(*Chapter 10: Wandering Rocks*)

This chapter comprises nineteen short scenes involving various Dubliners in different parts of the city; it is an 'odyssey within an odyssey'. In a few of the scenes we see Bloom and Stephen, who have both left the library and are looking at books on open stalls near the Liffey. The longest scenes in this episode are the first and last. The first section describes a walk taken by Father John Conmee, former rector of Stephen's school, Clongowes Wood, and the last section, the progress of the viceregal cavalcade from Phoenix Park in northwest Dublin to a bazaar at the Royal Dublin Society in Ballsbridge in the southeast part of the city.

The maps that follow detail the routes of both Father Conmee and the viceregal cavalcade, representing the spiritual and temporal powers that held sway in Dublin in 1904 – the Roman Catholic Church and the British government. It also shows the routes of the minor characters, each marked by the appropriate section number from the 'Wandering Rocks' episode. The nineteen episodes are summarised below.

1. This is Father Conmee's journey from the **Presbytery** (priest's residence) of the **Church of St Francis Xavier** on Upper Gardiner Street to the **O'Brien Institute** where he hopes to find a home for the orphaned son of Paddy Dignam. It consists of a 'walk to Artane' (10:3) and a ride on a tram (more commonly called a trolley car in the United States). He goes around '**Mountjoy square**' (10:12) by the 'treeshade of sunnywinking leaves' (10:16-17), turns left on 'Great Charles street' (10:69) and right into 'North Circular road' (10:73-74). Actually, the turn-of-the-century maps show this road as Richmond Place, but today it is part of North Circular Road. He passes Richmond Street, a short, dead-end road where he encounters a group of students from the Christian Brothers' **O'Connell School** (which James Joyce himself briefly attended in 1893) on the corner. North Circular Road becomes Portland Row, where Conmee passes **St Joseph's Roman Catholic Church** (10:79-80) and St Joseph's Asylum for Aged and Virtuous Females – now just called **St Joseph's Home for Aged**

Females – at 4-8 Portland Row. He next passes '**Aldborough House**' (10:83), one of the last Palladian mansions built in Ireland, now (as in 1904) owned and occupied by the Irish Post Office and devoid of its previous splendour. Conmee turns left onto North Strand Road and is 'saluted' (10:86) by Mr William Gallagher, who stands in the doorway of his grocery shop at No. 4 North Strand Road. Conmee also passes on North Strand Road Grogan's tobacconist's at No. 16, Daniel Bergin's Pub at No. 17, Youkstetter's porkbutcher shop at No. 21, and, on the opposite side of the street, H. J. O'Neill's funeral establishment (the firm that handled the Dignam burial) at No. 164 – all of which have since been demolished for public housing.

He crosses the **Royal Canal** at '**Newcomen bridge**' (10:107) where he boards a tram because he 'disliked to traverse on foot the dingy way past Mud Island' (10:113-114). The part of Dublin Bay to Father Conmee's right, which was mud flats in 1904, has been filled in to make **Fairview Park**. Conmee completes his tram journey, alighting at the 'Howth road stop' (10:153), to make the rest of his journey by foot *via* the 'quiet' (10:155) Malahide Road to the **O'Brien Institute for Destitute Children** (whose grounds contain the beautifully restored Georgian Marino Casino, a garden pavilion built by the English architect, William Chambers, for Lord Charlemont).

2.   Corny Kelleher is seen spitting and talking to a policeman while he works at H. J. O'Neill's undertaker's establishment at 164 North Strand Road.

3.   The map shows the path of a one-legged sailor (first seen outside the **Sisters of Charity Convent**, 76 Upper Gardiner Street, where he accosts Father Conmee – 10:9-10) along Dorset Street and Eccles Street, passing MacConnell's corner, named for Andrew MacConnell, pharmaceutical chemist at 112 Lower Dorset Street. The site is now a grocery store called The Corner Shop. He passes the Bloom residence at No. 7 Eccles Street, where Molly tosses him a coin (10:253). He then turns left into Nelson Street, where he is last seen (10:1063).

4.   This scene takes plact at No. 7 St Peter's Terrace (now renumbered **No. 5 St. Peter's Road**), Cabra, the home of the Joyce family in June 1904, just across the road from St. Peter's Church, Phibsborough. Stephen's sisters, Katey and Boody, have walked home from school by way of Eccles Street, Berkeley Road, North Circular Road and Cabra Road. They are seen with another sister, Maggy, washing shirts and complaining about how little money the family has. Boody mentions their sister Dilly, who has gone to

find their 'father who art not in heaven' (10:291).

5.   Molly's lover, Blazes Boylan, buys port, potted meat and fruits for her from Thornton's (10:299), a fruit shop and florist at No. 63 Grafton Street, now part of Dunne's Stores Ltd. Afterwards, he walks down Grafton Street, pauses outside La Maison Claire (10:984), dressmaker, at No. 4 (now a cakeshop, The Crusty Kitchen) and on towards Trinity College.

6.   Carrying his ashplant, Stephen meets his music teacher, Almidano Artifoni, at the **Trinity College** front gates opposite the 'blind columned porch' (10:342) of the **Bank of Ireland**, both magnificent buildings dating from the early 1700s. After a short conversation, Artifoni hastens toward an outgoing Dalkey tram, which he misses.

7.   The scene depicted is Blazes Boylan's office in central Dublin, probably The Advertising Co. at No. 15 D'Olier Street (the premises now shared by one of the *Irish Times* offices and a photography studio), where the secretary, Miss Dunne, types and answers a telephone call from Boylan.

8.   Ned Lambert shows a clergyman, Rev. Hugh C. Love, 'the most historic spot in all Dublin' (10:409): the old meeting room or chapter house of **St. Mary's Abbey**, 'where Silken Thomas proclaimed himself a rebel in 1534' (10:408-409). In 1904 Alexander seed merchants had a warehouse and offices at 2-5 Mary's Abbey (now **Clein's Carpets**), which included the old chapter house, all that was left of the once eminent monastery complex. Recently restored, the chapter house should be open to visitors on a regular basis starting in 1988.

9   The insert map shows the path of two minor characters, Lenehan and M'Coy, as they walk from Crampton Court to Capel Street Bridge. This is a very odd route to their destination, the **Ormond Hotel**. The two talk and Lenehan reminisces about Molly Bloom. Leaving Crampton Court, just south of the Capel Street Bridge, the two turn left onto Dame Street passing 'Dan Lowry's musichall' (10:495), officially the Empire Palace Theatre, at No. 72, and now called the **Olympia Theatre**, Dublin's oldest and most famous music hall. They take another left just past the theatre onto Sycamore Street, which runs into Essex Street East. Trying to find out what time it is, M'Coy looks into the 'sombre' office of Marcus Tertius Moses (10:508), a wholesale tea and wine merchant at 30 Essex Street East, and then into the shop of another tea and wine merchant, J. J. O'Neill, on the opposite corner at 29 Essex Street East (both no longer there). Essex

Street East becomes Temple Bar. They go under **Merchants' Arch**, a partly-covered passageway from Temple Bar to Wellington Quay on the south side of the Liffey, where they see Bloom.

10 Here we see Bloom at a bookshop, probably Fitzgerald's, at 1 Merchants' Arch, borrowing *Sweets of Sin* for Molly. This site is still a bookshop, today called **Ha'penny Bridge Books**, where the modern follower of Bloom might purchase, not borrow as he did, a secondhand copy of *Sweets of Sin*.

11 Outside Dillon's Auction Rooms (today the **Pierrot Snooker Club**), at No. 25 Bachelor's Walk, Stephen's sister Dilly asks her father for some money and whether he has been in a nearby pub. Simon Dedalus criticizes her posture and says, 'I'll leave you all where Jesus left the jews' (10:697-698). He gives her one shilling and two pence and walks off in the direction of the 'subsheriff's office' on Ormond Quay.

12. This section charts the course of Tom Kernan 'from the **sundial**' (10:718) at the junction of James's Street and Bow Lane West to the Liffey via James's and Watling streets. The sundial is there, but the other business premises Mr. Kernan passes on James's Street (Crimmins at 27, Shackleton at 35 and Kennedy at 48) are no longer there; however, as of 1988, the premises of 48 James's Street are still occupied by a Kennedy, this one being in the fish and poultry business while his namesake in 1904 was a hairdresser. Kernan sees from a distance the **Church of St Catherine** on Thomas Street, where the Irish patriot Robert Emmet was executed by the British government for his part in the abortive rising of 1803. He then goes by the former site of the **Guinness Brewery** visitors' waiting room (10:774) on the corner of James's and Watling streets (a site now occupied by the Bank of Ireland) and the 'stores' (10:775) of the Dublin Distillers Co. (the sign on the warehouse now reads 'The Central Hide & Skin Co., Ltd.') at 21-32 Watling Street.

13 The narrative now turns to Stephen's walk along Fleet Street, turning right onto 'Bedford Row' (10:830). He is first seen looking in the window of Thomas Russell, a gem cutter at 57 Fleet Street (since demolished to make way for the Dublin office of the Electricity Supply Board). He stops at Clohissey's bookstore at 10-11 Bedford Row to look at books and at a print of a bare-knuckle boxing match in 1860 that lasted thirty-seven rounds (10:831-835). He meets his sister Dilly who has crossed over the Liffey to spend some of the money her father gave her on a 'French primer' (10:867-868).

WANDERING ROCKS

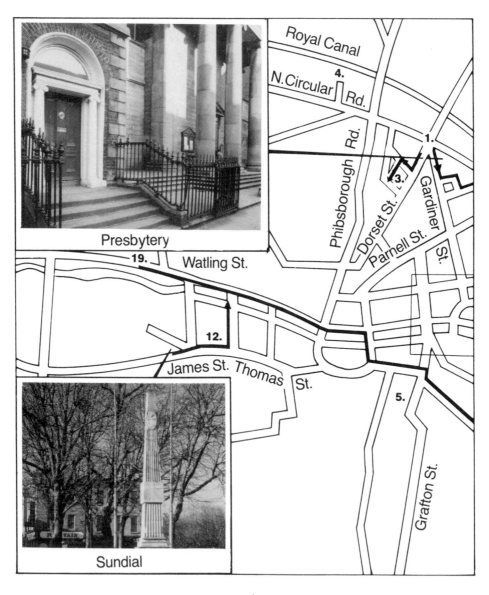

Presbytery

Watling St.

Sundial

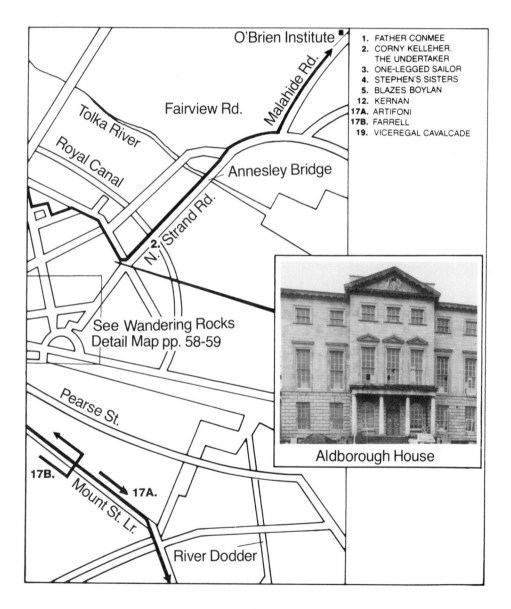

O'Brien Institute

Malahide Rd.

Fairview Rd.

Tolka River

Royal Canal

Annesley Bridge

N. Strand Rd.

2.

See Wandering Rocks
Detail Map pp. 58-59

Pearse St.

17B.

Mount St. Lr.

17A.

River Dodder

1. FATHER CONMEE
2. CORNY KELLEHER.
   THE UNDERTAKER
3. ONE-LEGGED SAILOR
4. STEPHEN'S SISTERS
5. BLAZES BOYLAN
12. KERNAN
17A. ARTIFONI
17B. FARRELL
19. VICEREGAL CAVALCADE

Aldborough House

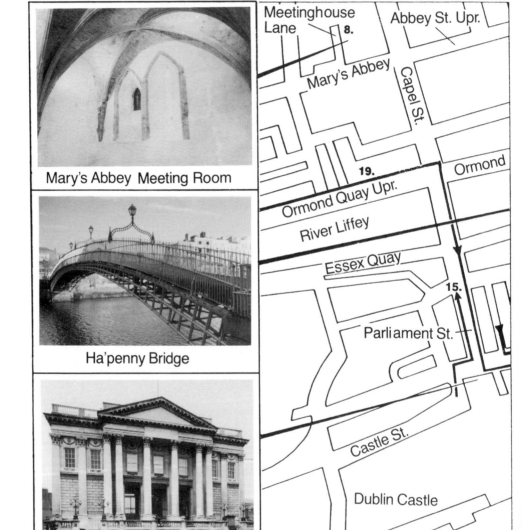

Mary's Abbey Meeting Room

Ha'penny Bridge

City Hall

WANDERING ROCKS DETAIL MAP

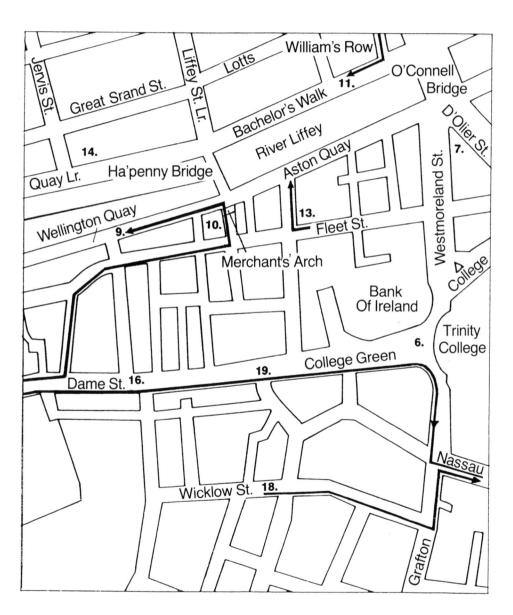

14. In this episode Simon Dedalus talks with two acquaintances, Cowley and Dollard, outside Reddy and Daughter's, an antique shop at 19 Lower Ormond Quay, near the Ormond Hotel. A visitor can still walk over the **'metal bridge'** (10:902) or **Ha'penny Bridge** (named for the toll needed to cross it centuries ago) where Ben Dollard comes 'at an amble, scratching actively behind his coattails' (10:903), to which Simon Dedalus cracks, 'Hold that fellow with the bad trousers' (10:905).

15. Next, we follow the short journey by Martin Cunningham and others from the courtyards of **Dublin Castle** to Kavanagh's Bar. Dublin Castle, the seat of British power in Ireland at the turn of the century, was attacked by members of the Irish Citizen Army during the 1916 Rising. Now, Irish governments use its grand eighteenth century ballrooms for presidential inaugurations and other state functions. Cunningham and his group walk from the Upper 'Castleyard gate' (10:957) on Castle Street to find a carriage. Cunningham signals to the driver to pick them up at the nearby intersection of Essex Gate and Parliament Street. They walk on up Castle Street and down Cork Hill, past the domed **City Hall**, still the seat of Dublin's city government. Going left into Parliament Street, they reach Kavanagh's Bar at 27 Parliament Street (now a pub called **Tommy Dunne's Tavern**).

16. In this section, Stephen's two room-mates at the Martello Tower, Mulligan and Haines, have cakes and scones at the Dublin Bread Company's tearoom at No. 33 Dame Street (since demolished). Mulligan repeats a familiar joke, that the restaurant is called DBC 'because they have damn bad cakes' (10:1058).

17. Stephen's music teacher, Artifoni, is walking near **Merrion Square** on Lower Mount Street, passing Holles Street and Sewell's Yard – then a livery stable for horses – at 60 Lower Mount Street. A well-known Dublin character named Cashel Boyle O'Connor Fitzmaurice Tisdall Farrell follows. He is a constant figure in Oliver Gogarty's *As I Was Going Down Sackville Street*. Farrell turns back at 'Mr Lewis Werner's cheerful windows' (10:1107), a Georgian townhouse at 31 Merrion Square North (then the offices of Louis Werner, ophthalmic surgeon) on the corner of Holles Street; he stops in front of the former home of Oscar Wilde's parents, who lived at No. 1 Merrion Square North (now the Dublin Document Exchange), and passes the poster in front of dingy **Merrion Hall** on Lower Merrion Street announcing the visit of an American evangelist. Farrell then crosses over onto Clare Street, strolling past 'Mr Bloom's dental windows' (10:1115), the offices of Marcus J. Bloom, dental

surgeon, No. 2 Clare Street (no relation to Leopold Bloom).

18.   Eager to leave a house filled with funeral mourners, Paddy Dignam's son, Patrick Aloysius, goes on an errand to pick up some pork-steaks from Mangan's butcher shop. Why he was sent almost two miles from their home on such an errand is never explained, but in any case we see him walking home from Mangan's at 1-2 South William Street (the building has apparently survived: the ground floor now houses the Impressions Boutique) *via* Wicklow Street, Grafton Street and Nassau Street. The butcher shop was located across the street from 'Ruggy O'Donohoe's' (10:1122), actually M. O'Donohoe, International Bar, 23 Wicklow Street, on the corner of St Andrew Street (now just known as the **International Bar**).

19.   This last section is the 'curtain call' for the chapter. As the viceregal procession passes, almost every character in the 'Wandering Rocks' chapter salutes the cavalcade. The British viceroy and his party go from the Viceregal Lodge in Phoenix Park (one of the oldest and largest city parks in the world) to attend the opening of the Mirus Bazaar in the **Royal Dublin Society** in Ballsbridge, a journey of about five miles.

The carriages leave the Phoenix Park at Park Gate and travel east along the quays that span the north side of the Liffey. The cavalcade crosses the Liffey at Capel Street Bridge, proceeds along Parliament Street, then turns left onto Dame Street, passes **Trinity College**, and, eventually crossing the Grand Canal at Mount Street Bridge, enters Ballsbridge *via* Northumberland and Pembroke roads.

The viceroy and his party pass the huge-domed **Four Courts** (10:1190) and the **Ormond Hotel** (10:1198). As the cavalcade crosses over Capel Street Bridge, it passes near to Dollard's Printing House at 2-5 Wellington Quay (still called **Dollard House**, but now with lawyers and accountants for tenants) and 'Roger Greene's office' (10:1205), a solicitor's office at No. 11 Wellington Quay, still occupied by **Roger Greene and Sons, Solicitors**.

Going up Parliament Street, the entourage passes Kavanagh's Bar (now called Tommy Dunne's Tavern). On Dame Street, it goes by the Marie Kendall poster at the Empire Palace (now **Olympia**) Theatre. Next passed on the route is 'King Billy's horse' (10:1232), a statue of King William III (the victor of the Battle of the Boyne in 1690) that once stood opposite **Trinity College** but has been replaced by a statue of the Irish patriot Thomas Davis. The cavalcade turns south onto Grafton Street and goes by 'Ponsonby's corner' (10:1236) – Edward Ponsonby, seller of legal and general books, government agent and contractor, at 116 Grafton Street (now a familiar stop for many American tourists since it houses the

Dublin branch of American Express), and by Pigott and Company at 112 Grafton Street. (The premises are now occupied by British Airways, but Pigott's still operates nearby as McCullough Pigott at 11-13 Suffolk Street.)

The carriages turn east (left) to Nassau Street, passing College Park in Trinity College and Finn's Hotel at 1-2 Leinster Street. (Joyce's wife, Nora, was working as a chambermaid at Finn's Hotel on June 16, 1904. Finn's Confectioners, a news-stand, now occupies the premises, but you can still see the name albeit faintly of Finn's Hotel on the Trinity College side of the building.) At the back gate of **Trinity College**, a porter touches his 'tallyho cap' (10:1264) in deference to the viceroy – the porters of Trinity College today wear an odd-looking hat reminiscent of the East German police.

Past Trinity College, Leinster Street becomes Clare Street and then Merrion Square North, where the young Dignam boy raises his cap. The route continues along Lower Mount Street and Northumberland Road past Haddington Road to the ultimate destination – Pembroke Road and the **Royal Dublin Society** (RDS) showgrounds, where the Mirus Bazaar was held. Today the Royal Dublin Society hosts one of the world's most famous horse shows in August, as well as many other cultural, sports and business events.

How to get there: Drive to O'Brien Institute or No. 27, 27a or 27b bus from Busarus to O'Brien Institute. Drive to Phœnix Park or No. 25 or 26 bus from Middle Abbey Street to Parkgate Street. Drive to Sundial or No. 78, 78a or 78b bus from Fleet Street to James's Street. Other sections: see locations on index map.

Park Gate, Phoenix Park, circa 1904.

Ballsbridge circa 1904.

Alex Findlater (on bike) halts the viceregal cavalcade outside Holles Street Hospital in a 1982 Bloomsday re-enactment of Chapter 10. Alexis Fitzgerald, then Lord Mayor of Dublin, played the part of the Viceroy. (Photo courtesy *The Irish Times*).

ORMOND HOTEL ON THE LIFFEY
3.38 p.m. to 4.40 p.m.
(*Chapter 11: Sirens*)

This chapter – the most 'musical' of *Ulysses* – is packed with song and music references and in style is based on the form of musical composition called a 'fugue', in which voices follow upon each other, taking up the same notes, rather like echoes chasing one another; this makes the chapter difficult to follow on first reading.

The action takes place almost entirely at the **Ormond Hotel** located at No. 8 Upper Ormond Quay on the River Liffey: this hotel, extensively remodelled since 1904, now has a bar called 'City Streets' and exhibits a plaque on the outside commemorating its fame as the setting for the Sirens episode. Apart from the activity within the hotel, there are three journeys associated with the chapter: Bloom's (and Boylan's) arrival; Boylan's ride to his assignation with Molly Bloom at No. 7 Eccles Street; and Bloom's departure for his appointment at the **Green Street Courthouse**.

Bloom is first seen on the south bank of the Liffey, just after he has emerged from **Merchants' Arch**. Joyce describes his walk: 'By Bassi's blessed virgins Bloom's dark eyes went by' (11:151). Today No. 14 Wellington Quay is still occupied by **A. Bassi & Co., Ltd.**, a religious goods store. Bloom wonders, 'Where eat? The Clarence, Dolphin. On' (11:188-189). The Dolphin Hotel is no more, but a Joycean today may still dine at the unpretentious **Clarence Hotel**, now expanded to include No. 8 as well as Nos. 6-7 Wellington Quay which it occupied in 1904. Deciding against either of these establishments, Bloom crosses over 'Essex bridge' (11:229 – since 1904 renamed Grattan Bridge but popularly known as **Capel Street Bridge**) and enters Daly's at No. 1 Upper Ormond Quay (today a bank occupies the site) to buy stationery. When he emerges, he sees jaunty Blazes Boylan on the bridge riding in a 'jaunting car' (11:302) and follows him to the Ormond Hotel.

Boylan pops into the bar for a quick drink ('sloegin' 11:350) and a word

SIRENS

....Boylan's Route   ■ Stopping Points

━━ Bloom's Route   ▪▪ Bloom's Projected Route

Ormond Hotel

in the ear of his crony, Lenehan. Bloom meets Richie Goulding (Stephen's uncle) and enters the dining room, choosing 'a table near the door' (11:391-392) in order to keep an ear, if not quite an eye, on the proceedings in the bar. He orders a 'bottle of cider' (11:447) and '[l]iver and bacon' (11:499) with 'liver gravy' and 'mashed potatoes' (11:553). In the meantime, Boylan departs, and the jingle of his jaunting car ride towards Molly keeps breaking into Bloom's thoughts as he drinks, eats and listens to the singing in the bar and surreptitiously writes an amorous letter to Martha Clifford. It is not clear whether the actual ride or Bloom's imagining of it is being described. All of the places mentioned as being passed by Boylan, including Graham Lemon's, Elvery's Elephant House (now a **Kentucky Fried Chicken** restaurant on the corner of O'Connell and Middle Abbey streets), the **statues** of Sir John Gray, Nelson and Father Mathew on O'Connell Street, the **Rotunda**, Dlugacz' butcher shop and Larry O'Rourke's pub have earlier in the day been passed and noticed by Bloom.

With the 'Cockcock' (11:988) of Boylan's proud knock on the door of No. 7 Eccles Street ringing in his mind's ear, Bloom gets up sadly to leave. Exiting the hotel, he turns right and heads towards the **Upper Ormond Quay post office** at No. 34 (still there as of 1988, but the adjoining buildings have been demolished) to buy a postal order to enclose with his letter to Martha. Thereafter, he will make his way to the **Green Street Courthouse**. The chapter ends, however, only a few doors west of the Ormond Hotel, outside 'Lionel Marks's antique saleshop window' (11:1261) at No. 16 Upper Ormond Quay (this window has since been bricked up), where, looking in, Bloom slowly breaks wind: the last, long and rather bass musical note.

Capel Street Bridge circa 1904.

How to get there: Within walking distance of O'Connell Street or take No. 79 (Ballyfermot) bus from Aston Quay to Heuston Bridge and walk back along the quays.

Clarence Hotel.

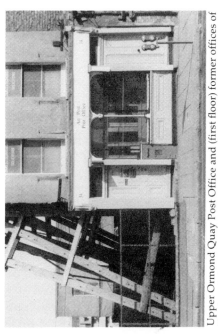

Upper Ormond Quay Post Office and (first floor) former offices of Reuben J. Dodd.

A. Bassi & Co. Ltd.

Formerly Lionel Marks's Saleshop window.

Barney Kiernan's Pub
4.45 p.m. to 5.45 p.m.
(Chapter 12: Cyclops)

Narrated by an unnamed Dublin debt collector, this chapter is set for the most part in Barney Kiernan's Pub, formerly located at 8-10 Little Britain Street. Bloom, having arrived at the Green Street Courthouse to meet Jack Power and Martin Cunningham by arrangement, at 5 o'clock sharp, finds that they are late; accordingly he passes the time by walking up and down the street outside the pub. Shortly thereafter, he is invited in. At the bar is 'the citizen', a character based on Michael Cusack (1847-1906), founder of the Gaelic Athletic Association. Bloom has a quarrel with this patriot concerning the Jewish religion, Irish politics, and whether Bloom should buy a round of drinks. Enraged, the citizen chases Bloom out and throws a biscuit tin at him, in a broad parody of the Cyclops episode in Homer's *Odyssey*.

The map on the opposite page details the route of the narrator and a friend: east from the Arbour Hill–Stoneybatter intersection (12:2) along North Brunswick Street, New Lisburn Street (no longer in existence) and Lisburn Street 'around by the Linenhall barracks' (12:64). They next turn right on either Linenhall Street or Lurgan Street (no way of telling which they take), down Halston Street passing 'the back of the courthouse' (12:64-65). The **Green Street Courthouse**, at 26 Green Street and running through to Halston Street, is now occupied by the Special Criminal Court, where many celebrated IRA suspects have been tried.

With its crowded markets and streets, this neighbourhood retains much of the atmosphere – if not the landmarks – of Joyce's Dublin. Barney Kiernan's Pub, reduced to two-thirds of its former size and without its bar fixtures, is a unisex barber shop called 'As You Like It'. The Linenhall Barracks are gone – as are the British soldiers they housed in 1904. Access to the Green Street Courthouse is usually restricted for security reasons.

How to get there: Take No. 37 (Ashtown) or No. 39 (Clonsilla) bus from Middle Abbey Street, to Stonybatter, Arbour Hill stop.

CYCLOPS

——Route of the Narrator and Hynes   ✳ No Longer A Through Street

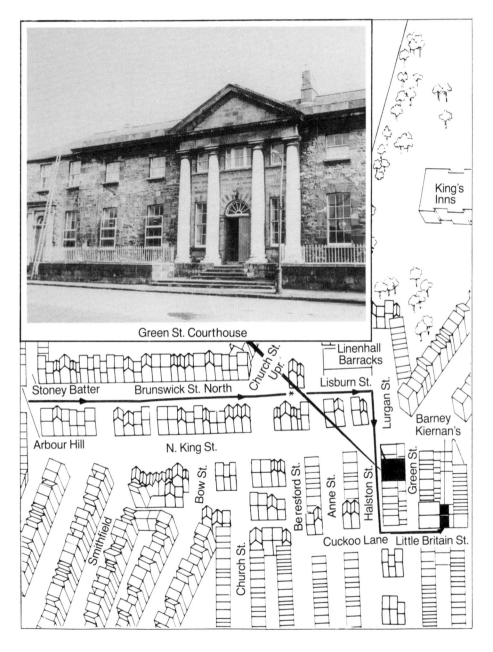

Green St. Courthouse

King's Inns

Stoney Batter   Brunswick St. North   Church St. Upr.   Linenhall Barracks

Lisburn St.   Lurgan St.

Barney Kiernan's

Arbour Hill   N. King St.

Bow St.   Beresford St.   Anne St.   Halston St.   Green St.

Smithfield   Church St.

Cuckoo Lane   Little Britain St.

SANDYMOUNT STRAND REVISITED
8.00 p.m. to 9.00 p.m.
(*Chapter 13: Nausicaa*)

After arriving at Paddy Dignam's house at **No. 9 Newbridge Avenue** in Sandymount shortly before 6.00 p.m., Bloom spends approximately two hours with Mrs. Dignam and agrees to help the family in settling the estate. He then strolls down to **Sandymount Strand**, the same beach along which Stephen walked in chapter 3. Partly styled as a parody of the popular romantic magazines of Joyce's time (Joyce called it a 'namby-pamby jamsy marmalady drawersy [*alto la!*] style with effects of incense, mariolatry, masturbation, stewed cockles, painter's palette, chitchat, circumlocution, etc., etc.'), this chapter starts with a scene describing three girls playing with some children on the beach. When Bloom arrives, one of the girls, Gerty MacDowell, realizes that he is watching her; she leans back to watch a fireworks display and purposely lets Bloom see under her dress. Bloom becomes sexually aroused, and at this point the style of the chapter changes. We now follow Bloom's stream of consciousness until the chapter ends as nine cuckoos are heard from a clock at the nearby 'priest's house' (13:1292), **No. 3 Leahy's Terrace**, across from the **Star of the Sea Church**.

The map on the opposite page shows the path taken by Bloom from Dignam's house to Sandymount Strand. Joyce made particular inquiries of his aunt Josephine about the trees in Leahy's Terrace and the steps leading down to the sea, evidence of his careful use of exact detail in the novel. Though the Leahy's Terrace steps of 1904 have disappeared, the **Star of the Sea Church** is still 'a beacon ever to the stormtossed heart of man' (13:7-8), albeit slightly more inland; and, appropriately, the Canon O'Hanlon Memorial National School has been built approximately on the spot where Bloom admired young Gerty's display. You can recreate the scene of Nausicaa by walking south from Leahy's Terrace along Beach Road past Marine Drive to the existing Sandymount Strand.

How to get there: DART train to Lansdowne Road station. Or take a No. 2 or No. 3 (Sandymount) bus from O'Connell Street to Leahy's Terrace (Star of the Sea Church) stop.

NAUSICAA

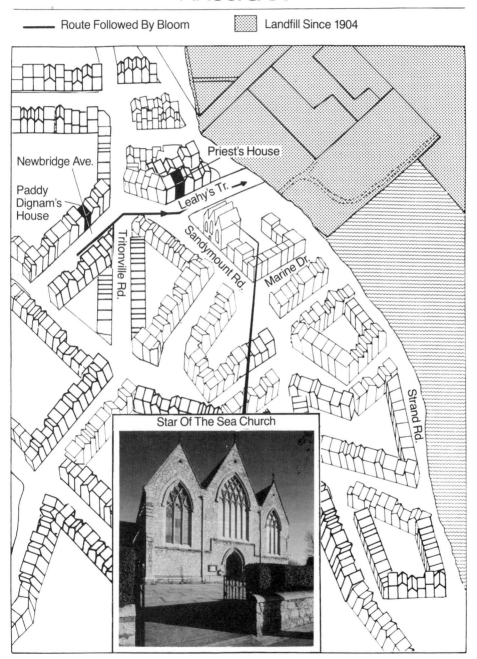

——— Route Followed By Bloom   ▓ Landfill Since 1904

Newbridge Ave.

Paddy Dignam's House

Priest's House

Leahy's Tr. →

Tritonville Rd.

Sandymount Rd.

Marine Dr.

Strand Rd.

Star Of The Sea Church

Holles Street Hospital
10.00 p.m. to 11.00 p.m.
(Chapter 14: Oxen of the Sun)

This chapter traces both the nine months of pregnancy and the various stages in the development of the English language. Bloom returns to the centre of Dublin probably *via* the Sandymount (Haddington Road) tram, which would drop him very close to the main entrance of the **National Maternity Hospital** in Holles Street. This hospital is still in existence (though totally rebuilt after Joyce's departure) and is where most of this episode takes place. It opens with Bloom inquiring at the hospital after his friend, Mrs. Purefoy, who has been three days in labour. Once again Bloom encounters Stephen Dedalus, who is at the hospital carousing with some medical students. Bloom decides to keep an eye on him. Buck Mulligan arrives late from the *soirée* at the writer George Moore's house at **No 4 Upper Ely Place** (this elegant Georgian building has since been marked with a plaque); and Haines, who like Mulligan has not been seen since they sat eating cakes in the D.B.C. in chapter 10, drops in momentarily to remind Mulligan to meet him at Westland Row station at 11.10 p.m. When the baby is delivered, just before 11.00 p.m., Stephen and his companions leave the hospital to have a nightcap at Burke's Pub, then on the corner of Holles Street and Denzille Street (now Fenian Street). After closing time at Burke's, Stephen and a friend named Lynch go to the **Westland Row station**, to take a train to **Amiens Street station**. Bloom follows Stephen to the hospital, pub and train station.

The map opposite shows the location of the **National Maternity Hospital** on Holles Street and the spot (today a flower shop) where Burke's Pub stood. It also details the route that Stephen (followed by Bloom) takes to get from Burke's Pub to the Westland Row station *via* Holles Street, Denzille Lane, Fenian Street, and Westland Row. At the Fenian Street-Lower Merrion Street intersection, the characters pass the dreary **Merrion Hall**, still today carrying a poster announcing our salvation as only of the Lord; hence the language with which the chapter closes: 'Shout salvation in King Jesus' (14:1588).

How to get there: Take No. 7 (Sallynoggin) or No. 8 (Dalkey) bus from Eden Quay to Lower Mount Street, Holles Street Hospital stop.

OXEN OF THE SUN

—— Route Of Stephen And Lynch Followed By Bloom — — — Projected Route

■ Stopping Point

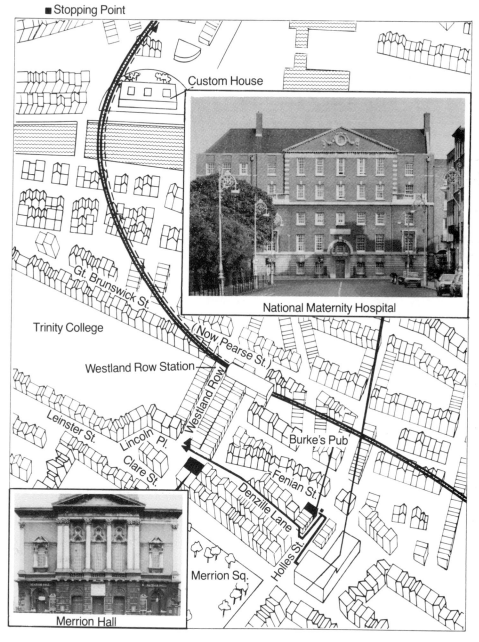

Custom House

National Maternity Hospital

Trinity College

Gt. Brunswick St.

Now Pearse St.

Westland Row Station

Westland Row

Leinster St.

Lincoln Pl.

Clare St.

Burke's Pub

Fenian St.

Denzille Lane

Holles St.

Merrion Sq.

Merrion Hall

NIGHTTOWN
11.15 p.m. to 1.00 a.m.
(*Chapter 15: Circe*)

At about a quarter past eleven, Stephen and Lynch walk from **Amiens Street station** to Bella Cohen's brothel *via* Talbot Street and Mabbot Street (now Corporation Street) or, in the opening words of the chapter, 'The Mabbot street entrance of nighttown' (15:1). Joyce apparently coined the term 'nighttown' to refer to this once-famous red-light district of Dublin. Most Dubliners would have called the area 'Monto' (after Montgomery Street); however, Joyce did not invent Bella Cohen – she was a real-life Dublin madam in 1904.

Bloom misses the stop at Amiens Street station and gets off at the next stop. By the time he returns to Amiens Street (presumably by the next incoming train), he somehow catches up with Stephen and Lynch at Bella Cohen's, 82 Lower Tyrone Street (since renamed Railway Street, perhaps to disguise its past history), where Stephen is playing the piano, drinking, and dancing. Leaving Bella Cohen's, and reaching the corner of Beaver Street, Stephen gets into an argument with two British soldiers. Bloom comes to Stephen's assistance, and the chapter ends with Bloom standing paternal guard over Stephen.

You should exercise caution in following the path from the **Amiens Street station** shown on the map. As in 1904, and although the brothels are gone, this is not Dublin's safest neighbourhood. Also, the names may confuse. The principal street, Lower Tyrone Street, where the brothels were literally side by side, was until 1887 called 'Mecklenburg Street' (15:109), and is now known as Railway Street; Mabbot Street is now Corporation Street, although Mabbot Lane is still Mabbot Lane; and Montgomery Street has been rechristened Foley Street. 'Purdon street' (15:611), formerly between and parallel to Tyrone and Montgomery Streets, and 'Faithful place' (15:91), a laneway opposite Mrs. Cohen's, are both gone, victims of the cleaning up of Nighttown in 1925 three years after the British garrison left Southern Ireland. Most of the once elegant houses and buildings are also gone and have been replaced by

CIRCE

━ Route Of Stephen Followed By Bloom

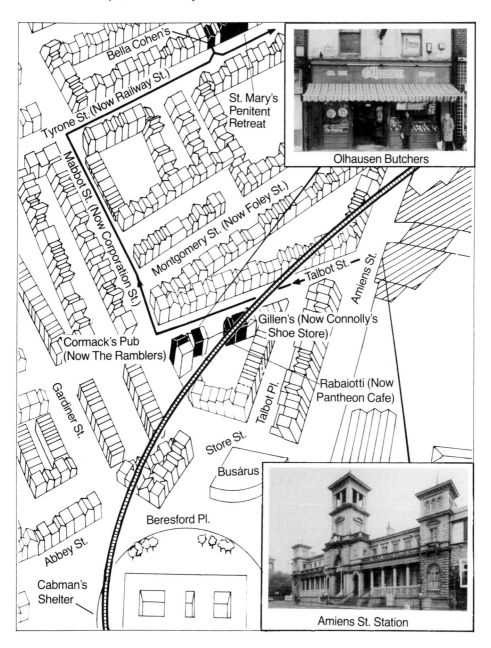

Olhausen Butchers

Amiens St. Station

unimaginative public housing projects.

Not everything has changed, however. To follow Bloom's footsteps, you should start at Amiens Street station, cross the road and walk down the left side of Talbot Street (still a busy commercial area) and under the railway bridge. This is the point where Bloom, carrying a fourpenny square of sodabread and a tablet of Fry's plain chocolate, first appears in the chapter (15:142-3). He examines his form, elongated and enlarged in the convex mirror, in the window of Gillen's hairdressers (now **Connolly's** shoe store) at No. 64 before entering Antonio Rabaiotti's fish-and-chip restaurant at No. 65 (today modernised and renamed the **Pantheon Café**, but still selling 'fish and taters'). Deciding against that fare, 'N.g.' (no good), Bloom steers into '**Olhausen's**, the porkbutcher's' (15:155) at No. 72 (it is still there!) to buy a pig's crubeen and a sheep's trotter (i.e. a cooked pig's foot and sheep's foot). At the corner of Mabbot Street he halts outside Thomas Cormack's pub (15:168 – today renamed **The Ramblers** Lounge) at No. 74, turns right and rushes across the road. In transit, he is grazed by two cyclists and nearly run down by a sandstrewer, whose driver addresses him in choice Dublinese (you will get the same if you are not more careful): 'Hey, shitbreeches, are you doing the hat trick?' (referring to Bloom's trio or 'hat trick' of near accidents – 15:195). Safely across, and on the right side of Mabbot (Corporation) Street, the hallucinations, for which this chapter is famous, begin: he spies a 'sinister figure' leaning against the wall of O'Beirne's Pub (now a vacant site) across the road at No. 26 Talbot Street.

Proceeding up Mabbot Street, Bloom meets a ragman, children, a dog, ghosts from his past, a bawd and Mrs. Breen, a friend to whom he must explain away his presence in the area. They part, probably at the corner of Purdon Street, and Bloom walks on, past noisy wrestling loiterers, while cheap whores 'call from lanes, doors, corners' (15:598). He tosses the crubeen and the trotter to the dog that has been following him and is approached by two suspicious policemen. There follows a phantasmagoric trial in which his guilty conscience conjures up yet more ghosts. By now he has turned into Lower Tyrone (Railway) Street and reaches Mrs. Cohen's at No. 82 (Joyce, for superstitious reasons, changes this to 81 – 15:1287), which at first he thinks is Mrs. Mack's, then at No. 85. Stephen is inside; Bloom enters. Both these dwellings are now gone, though two doors away, at Nos. 68-80, the convent which housed St Mary's Penitent Retreat, a laundry where reformed prostitutes worked, still stands. The part of the convent on Gloucester (now Sean MacDermott) Street was in 1904 known as St Mary Magdalen's Asylum, for which Bloom falsely claimed to Mrs. Breen that he was the secretary (15:402); it is now known as the **Gloucester Street Convent and Laundry** of the Sisters of Our Lady of Charity.

On leaving, Stephen is first out, running (15:4256), and speeds down Tyrone Street to the corner of Beaver Street, where he gets into an argument with two English soldiers. Beaver Street today is little more than a laneway, and the visitor should not linger on its lonely corner. Bloom follows, and as the chapter ends, stands over Stephen who is lying semi-conscious on the ground.

The Mabbot Street entrance of Nighttown as it is today.

How to get there: DART to Amiens Street station.

The North Star Hotel.

Dan Bergin's pub (now Lloyd's).

Mullett's bar – still at No. 45 Amiens Street.

The Ramblers (formerly Cormack's Corner).

Signal House (now J. & M. Cleary).

CABMAN'S SHELTER
1.00 a.m. to 2.00 a.m.
(Chapter 16: Eumaeus)

Written in a rambling, wordy style evocative of the characters' weariness and the lateness of the hour, this chapter opens with Bloom helping Stephen off the pavement at the corner of Tyrone and Beaver streets. The two then go to a cabman's shelter, described as an 'unpretentious wooden structure' (16:321), catering primarily to drivers of horse-drawn vehicles. Bloom buys Stephen a coffee and bun, and they listen to an old sailor telling stories. Both are tired, and they begin their walk to Bloom's house (about a mile away) as the chapter ends.

The cabman's shelter no longer exists, but you will pass many buildings from Joyce's era by taking Stephen and Bloom's path from Lower Tyrone Street (now Railway Street) to the cabman's shelter. They walked together along Beaver Street past the farriers and towards the livery stables at the corner of Montgomery (Foley) Street. (Both these businesses are long gone.) Turning left, they reach 'Dan Bergin's' Pub (16:24 – now **Lloyd's Lounge Bar**) at the corner of Amiens Street, where Bloom sees in the distance a cab outside the '**North Star hotel**' (16:27), still located at 26-30 Amiens street. Bloom's weak whistling fails to attract the cab, so the pair walk on, past '**Mullett's**', still at No. 45, and the 'Signal House' (16:33-34), now **Cleary's Pub**, at No. 36 Amiens Street. They go by the '**Amiens street railway terminus**' (16:35), the 'backdoor of the morgue' (16:48 – the **Dublin City Morgue** at 2-4 Amiens Street, still there), and the Dock Tavern, now the **Master Mariner Bar**, on the corner of Amiens and Store streets. In their journey they also pass the police station at No. 3 and the City Bakery (now **Kylemore Bakery, Ltd.**) at Nos. 5-6 Store Street. The cabman's shelter was near the **Custom House** which was gutted during the 1921 'Troubles', but which has since been carefully rebuilt.

How to get there: Within walking distance of O'Connell Street.

EUMAEUS

━━━ Route Of Stephen And Bloom

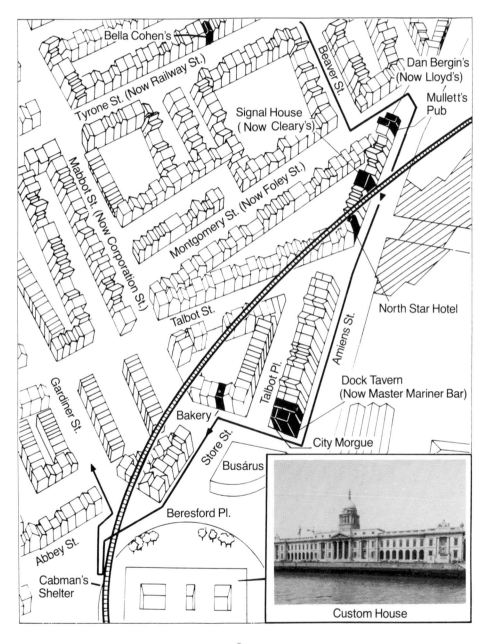

Custom House

HOME
2.00 a.m. to 2.45 a.m.
(*Chapter 17: Ithaca*)

This chapter, which opens with Bloom and Stephen walking to Bloom's house at No. 7 Eccles Street, is written in a question-and-answer style reminiscent of a catechism. Arriving at his house, Bloom finds he has forgotten to take a house key and must climb over a railing and lower himself to a basement-level door to get into his house. Joyce's friend, John Byrne (the Cranly of *Portrait of the Artist*), lived on Eccles Street and once let Joyce into his house in this way. Bloom takes Stephen down to the kitchen and gives him some cocoa. Stephen refuses the offer of a place to stay for the night and departs. Bloom gets ready for bed; then, lying alongside but in the opposite direction to his wife Molly, he tells her about some of the day's activities, not totally accurately, but not fooling Molly either.

The map shows Stephen and Bloom's route from the cabman's shelter. Joyce describes it in the first question and answer in the episode:

What parallel courses did Bloom and Stephen follow returning?

Starting united both at normal walking pace from **Beresford place** they followed in the order named **Lower and Middle Gardiner streets** and **Mountjoy square**, west: then, at reduced pace, each bearing left, **Gardiner's place** by an inadvertence as far as the farther corner of **Temple street**: then, at reduced pace with interruptions of halt, bearing right, Temple street, north, as far as **Hardwicke place**. Approaching, disparate, at relaxed walking pace they crossed both the circus before **George's church** diametrically, the chord in any circle being less than the arc which it subtends (17:1-10). (Emphasis mine.)

Later, after shaking hands with Bloom, Stephen, passing through the door in the backyard wall of No. 7 Eccles Street onto an adjoining lane, exits from 'Ithaca' and from literature. Presumably, he makes his way along the lane back onto Eccles Street and thence to his father's house, not far distant, following the same route that his sisters took in chapter 10 (see page 53). The last that is heard of him is 'The double reverberation of retreating feet on the heavenborn earth, the double vibration of a jew's harp in the resonant lane' (17:1243-4).

ITHACA

Route Of Stephen And Bloom

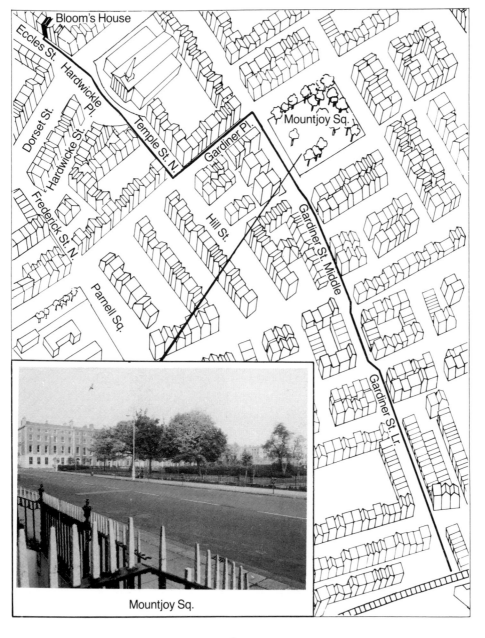

Mountjoy Sq.

85

Molly's Bed
About 2.00 a.m. to 2.17 a.m.
(Chapter 18: Penelope)

Joyce gives Molly Bloom the last word, bringing *Ulysses* to an end with her famous soliloquy: in Joyce's own words, 'the indispensible countersign to Bloom's passport to eternity'. All the action, such as it is, takes place in 'the lumpy old jingly bed' (18:1212), in which Molly lies awake daydreaming, leaving it only briefly. She journeys back over the events of the day to more distant memories of her youth. The bed itself has come with her on the odyssey that was her life: 'All the way from Gibraltar' (4:60). Her father, Major Brian Tweedy, had bought it off 'old Cohen' (18:1213), although Molly told Bloom that he got it from 'Lord Napier' (18:1214) 'at the governor's auction' (4:62). Since that far-off day in the Mediterranean sun, it became for the Blooms 'the bed of conception and of birth, of consummation of marriage and of breach of marriage' (17:2119-20) and followed them from 'Raymond terrace and Ontario terrace and Lombard street and Holles street' and the 'City Arms hotel' (18:1216-20) to Eccles Street.

The map on the opposite page shows some of the places in Dublin Molly mentions in her soliloquy: **Westland Row chapel** (18:709), where Molly remembers seeing Stephen; **Switzer's** (18:1045), still a thriving department store; and the **National Museum** 'in Kildare street' (18:1202).

The final map shows most of the places in Gibraltar that Molly remembers from her youth. (Note how the peninsula bears a striking resemblance to the head of James Joyce.) There is, for example: O'Hara's Tower, near where she says she would like 'a new fellow every year up on the tiptop near the rockgun' (18:781-2); Windmill Hill that she went up one Sunday morning with Captain Rubios to the Flats (18:856-7); the Alameda Gardens that have 'the glorious sunsets and the figtrees' (18:1599) and where she was kissed 'under the Moorish wall' (18:1604) in Gibraltar as a girl.

PENELOPE

1. National Museum
2. Westland Row Chapel
3. Switzer's Window, Grafton St.

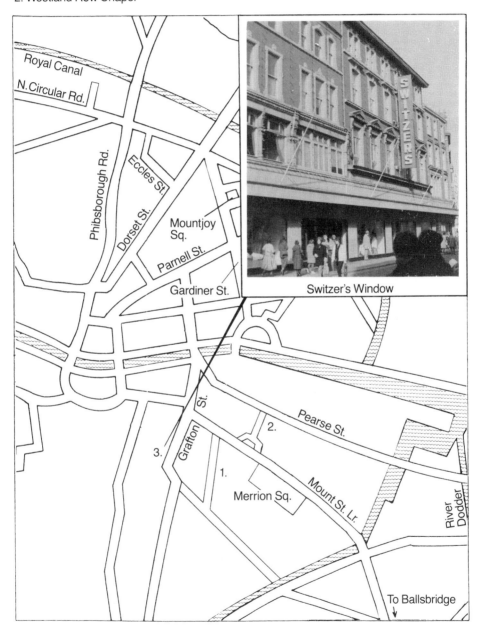

Switzer's Window

GIBRALTAR

The map opposite shows the principal features of the Rock and most of the places remembered by Molly Bloom in her soliloquy.

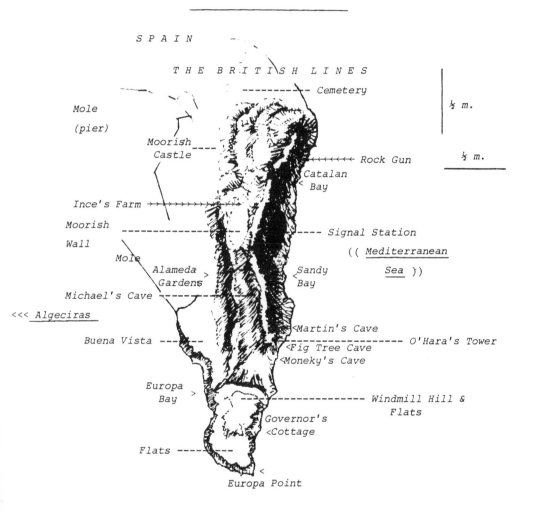

GIB

(Calpe)

SPAIN

THE BRITISH LINES

Cemetery

½ m.

Mole

(pier)

Moorish
Castle

Rock Gun

½ m.

Catalan
< Bay

Ince's Farm →→→→→→→→

Moorish

Wall

Signal Station

((Mediterranean

Mole

Sea))

Alameda
Gardens >

<Sandy
Bay

Michael's Cave

<<< Algeciras

<Martin's Cave

Buena Vista

O'Hara's Tower

<Fig Tree Cave

<Moneky's Cave

Europa
Bay >

Windmill Hill &
Flats

Governor's
<Cottage

Flats

<
Europa Point

THE STRAITS SHINING

Apes' Hill
(Abyla)
AFRICA

INDEX

An index to some Joycean places still to be seen in Dublin (as of 1988),
and referred to in this book.

Some Reviewers' Comments

JOYCE'S DUBLIN
A Walking Guide to *Ulysses*
JACK McCARTHY

'Like an accomplished raconteur . . . McCarthy drops in various items
of biographical, historical or merely local interest. . . . The author has
provided a convenient skeleton review of the Dublin of *Ulysses*, leaving
at least this reader with a yearning to return again.'
Richard M. Kain in *James Joyce Literary Supplement*

'Here at last is the sort of book which every amateur
Joycean visitor to Dublin has been looking for.'
James Joyce Broadsheet (Leeds, England)

'Anything but the usual academic tome that American devotees
of James Joyce seem to churn out interminably.'
Irish Independent (Dublin)

'Jack McCarthy has come to your rescue with a wonderful project.'
Irish Edition (Philadelphia)

———————

— JOYCEAN VIDEO —
Walking Into Eternity: James Joyce's Ulysses – A Dublin Guide with Patrick Ryan
– a 28-minute film documentary produced and directed
by Emmy award winner Seán Ó Mordha.

International Sales Contact:
The Ryan Group of Princeton Inc., 228 Alexander Street, P.O. Box 2329
Princeton, New Jersey 08543-2329, United States of America
Telephone: (609) 924-1199

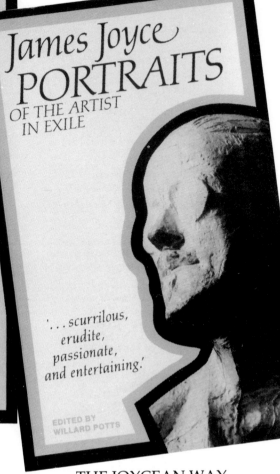

Portraits of the Artist in Exile
Recollections of James Joyce by Europeans

'In this well-edited and attractively produced volume Professor Potts has collected memoirs and miscellaneous commentaries on Joyce by friends, associates and casual interviewers in Trieste, Zürich, Paris and other European centres . . .'
The Irish Press

'Once again we are indebted to an American for a worthwhile edition to Joyce's scholarship . . . These recollections span the entire period from his arrival in Pola in 1904 at the age of twenty-two until his death in Zurich two weeks short of his fifty-ninth birthday: beginning with Francini Bruni's high spirited picture of the young Berlitz school teacher and ending with the moving valediction written after Joyce's death by Paul Leon, his devoted helper and friend.'
Niall Sheridan, Hibernia

'This omnium gatherum will be extraordinarily helpful for those interested in Joyce's biography . . . . The writers of these essays are names possibly familiar to us from Ellmann's *Life* where references are made to Joyce's friends and acquaintances like Nino Frank, . . . Jan Parandowski, . . . Paul Ruggiero. But here are the actual recollections, showing a wide range in tone, insight and literary style.'
Irish University Review

Cover design: Jan de Fouw.
Cover illustration shows a plastercast of a bronze statue of James Joyce by Milton Hebalt. Photo courtesy Bord Fáilte.

WOLFHOUND PRESS

68 Mountjoy Square, Dublin 1.
£5.95 ISBN 0-86327-026-3 paperback

THE JOYCEAN WAY

For his party piece, James Joyce used to recite the names of all the shops in O'Connell Street, Dublin. Even in his exile, the city of Dublin remained the centre of his universe. Alongside its buildings, backstreets, thoroughfares and suburbs, Joyce steered his literary course to genius.

In this book, by means of photographs, maps and close textual examination, the authors chart the fascination that Dublin held for Joyce and the movements of Joyce's characters through it. In *The Joycean Way*, the city lives as it does in *Dubliners* and *A Portrait of the Artist*, revealing to the reader a composite interface of people and places. Any reader of Joyce, or lover of Dublin, will welcome this guide to the city of Joyce's masterpieces.